"Thank you so much for w
pecially touched by the d........ between Joshua and his dad
while Joshua was away...it's helped me to speak to my heavenly
Dad."
—Carolyn Morrison

"*Like Father Like Son* is awesome. It just made what Christ did
for us so plain and open and simple for anyone to understand, if
they are wanting to know."
—Gail

"Your book ministered so deeply to me. As I read it, I was constantly thinking of my family. God is going to use what He has
given you concerning fathers and fatherhood more and more. It
is a message to the Church whose time has come, and it will
play a major role in what God is going to do worldwide in the
months and years ahead. I have seen Jesus and the Holy Spirit
personified to the Church. Now the Father's time is at hand."
—Pastor Ed Carlson

"I so much enjoyed the book. It showed a wonderful relationship of God's love toward His Son. I don't believe C.S. Lewis
could have written it better. The style reminded me a lot of his
fictional books."
—William S. Rundell

"I finished *Like Father Like Son* before I returned home. Wow!
What a terrific story."
—Bill Lee

LIKE FATHER
Like Son

A Parable

Robert J. LaCosta

ISBN 1-58169-102-5
For Worldwide Distribution
Printed in the U.S.A.

Second printing 2004

Gazelle Press
P.O. Box 191540 • Mobile, AL 36619
800-367-8203

ROBERT J. LaCOSTA is an author, speaker, and a singer/songwriter who resides in upstate New York.

For booking information,
contact No Reputation Communications
at 518-435-1400,
fax request to 518-435-0020,
or email to noreputations@aol.com.

A portion of the profits from this printing are going to:
Hearts of the Father Outreach, Inc.: an organization that serves orphans in the real "City of Children" places throughout the world.

Acknowledgments

I wish to thank Father God, Son Jesus Christ, and the Holy Spirit for writing this parable on my heart. To my earthly parents, Paul and Lucy LaCosta, who viewed me as a beloved son instead of judging me as a child who had mountains and valleys. To my father-in-law, Harry Krusch, who brought me into his family as a son. To my brother Paul, who helped me understand and honor my father.

To Royal A. Cutler, who in leading me through the Word of God, did not allow his brilliant mind to block the heart lessons that he had learned from his Heavenly Father. May I have this reality in my spiritual genetics. To Mary Elizabeth, "Davey," his beloved wife, who is a writer and has encouraged me through the years with unrelenting truths and their accompanying security. To Pastor Stephen P. Lalor and his wife, Karen, who have brought us up in the faith. I remember so well the day that I left for my first writer's conference and how Pastor pressed a generous gift into my palm as a "seed" for his son. May it yield a mighty harvest.

To brothers and sisters and in-laws, Mary Ann and Michael D'Arco, Lucille and Tony Davino, Paula LaCosta, Paul and Susan LaCosta, Jessica, Kelli, Lucy, Maggie and Paul; to John LaCosta who sent me an Italian pen that turned out to be a sign from the Lord; to John's wife, Danette and their children, John, Nicholas, and Isabella; to Michael LaCosta and his children Erin and Michael. One could wish for no finer family. To my spiritual brother, Daniel Baggott, for his love for me; to his wife, Lee, and their children, Scott and Jessica. For Marlene Bagnull, who encourages writers—no matter what stage they're

v

at. May our Father open His floodgates to you and your work. To Tim Bennett, friend and author who encouraged me and went where I needed to follow. To Tim Madden, who has greatly influenced my fathering by following his Heavenly Father. To the many editors and readers over the years who have said kind words regarding my writing. It helps. I'd like to thank my wife, Bettina, for understanding that writing is part of my DNA and not wishing that I'd been created in some other fashion. To my daughter, Guinevere, who started me out in this business of fathering, not minding being the first in this laboratory of love. Finally, I would like to thank my daughter Angelique: Your wide eyes encouraged me every time I started to tuck you in with the words, "There once was..."

Dedication

This work is dedicated to my Heavenly Father and His Son,
Jesus Christ, who both taught me how to be a son.

To my earthly father, Paul F. LaCosta, Sr.,
whose kisses sent me off and welcomed me back.
I'm eager to know that joy again.

To my spiritual father, Dr. Royal A. Cutler, Jr.,
who fathered my understanding of the scriptures.

And to my pastoral father, Stephen P. Lalor,
who fathered my confidence.

To my wife, Bettina,
who has understood
that fathering is an art that I am still learning.

To my children, Guinevere and Angelique,
who have given me a measure
of my Heavenly Father's perspective.

To my son-in-law, in whose eyes I see the longing
of his name, Benjamin.

Preface

The following parable had its beginnings in a humble bedtime story when my daughters were young. It was meant to allegorize the simplicity of the Gospel. Toward the end, one of them sat up in bed and said, "Oh, now I get it!" Call it a simple man's "Fifth Gospel," or a 160-page tract. Whatever it is, may we all become like children who "get it" and in so doing, become like Father.

Foreword

The author has written an imaginative parable of the age old conflict between good and evil. I was drawn into the story and found it hard to put the book down until I discovered how it all turned out.

Bob LaCosta and I have been in somewhat of a father/son relationship for over fifteen years, and I have seen him mature and move in his gifts. Obviously writing is one of them, and I believe he has done a fine job. I highly recommend this book as a "good read."

—*Royal A. Cutler, Jr.*

It was his father's eyes. It was his dad's generosity.
It was the view from the cliff. These three things
stirred Joshua's heart.

CHAPTER ONE

"Dad," Joshua said, "you promised me a camping trip. Can we go soon?"

His dad brushed off his sleeves and looked at his son. He yanked at the reigns and guided the horse toward the barn while Joshua tagged along.

"Are you up for it, son?" his father asked.

"I'm up for it!" Joshua exclaimed.

A smile slowly developed from the corner of his dad's lips.

"Is that a 'Yes'?" Joshua asked.

"That's a big 'Yes,'" his dad said as two young arms wrapped around his waist. "That's a real big 'Yes.'"

"Have you been waiting for me to ask?" Joshua inquired.

"I knew it would happen at the right time," his father said. "Your twelfth birthday is this week. I can't think of a better time for our outing. Perfect weather, too."

His father sniffed the spring air and called for one of the ranch's servants.

"Would you look after the left front hoof?" his father asked as he stroked the white stallion. "I think it needs some attention."

"Yes, sir," said the servant with the kind of reply that one can trust. "I'll take good care of him. He always takes good care of you."

"Thanks, Charlie," his father said to the servant.

After supper, Joshua found himself in his father's den sitting

1

in a companion chair to the one his dad used. It was too big for him, but he loved that chair. It put him close to his dad. Only the oil lamp separated their chairs. The fireplace was just a few feet away. Its heat was just enough to take a slight chill out of the room.

"What are you writing about?" Joshua asked.

His dad slowly took his eyes off the paper and looked at Joshua in the oversized chair.

"I'm writing in my journal about how your heart and mind have grown."

"Dad," Joshua said, "you're always thinking about me and others. Don't you ever think of yourself?"

"Only about how blessed I am to have you and this beautiful ranch," his dad replied.

Joshua came over and sat in his dad's lap.

"I almost thought you were too big for this," Dad joked.

"Well, I hope your lap is always big enough for me," Joshua said.

"As long as you never get too big for it," his dad smiled, "there will always be room on my lap for you."

Joshua was rather tall for his age, and his legs dangled off the side of the chair. He began to feel very comfortable and promptly fell asleep. He dreamed of the horse ride to the backside of the woods of the ranch. He and his dad were racing their horses to the cliff. The air was cool and blew his hair back. When he awoke, the wind from his bedroom window was actually blowing on his face.

"But it was so real," Joshua said to his sleepy self.

He looked up at the ceiling. His dad had painted stars over his bed when he was young. They seemed so deep and far away. It made him feel that they were inviting him to travel far away from the security of his bedroom.

He got up and remembered the camping trip and went scurrying downstairs, tousled hair, sleepy eyes and all.

Will dad want to take me today? he thought.

"Where's dad?" he asked Mrs. Wooster, their stout and stocky red-haired cook.

"Well, master," she replied with a slight smile, "not even a good morning?"

"I'm sorry," Joshua said. He came over and gave her the hug that she was used to receiving.

"Now that's better!" she said. "Where do you think he is?"

She winked at him.

Joshua started for the door, but was stopped as a strong and stubby hand grabbed his arm.

"Not so fast, Master Joshua," said Mrs. Wooster. "You must sit down and eat."

"But I've got to talk to him," Joshua said. The words spilled out of his mouth so fast that Mrs. Wooster could hardly understand him.

"He'll be back in a minute," she said. "Go up and get washed up. By that time, he'll be back from the barn and the two of you can have a pre-birthday breakfast feast. I've been cookin' up a storm for you, my young master. Now, go ahead!"

She gave Joshua a playful shove toward the stairs.

Joshua caught another of her winks, sniffed the aroma of the pancakes, and thought about the barn.

"O.K.!" he exclaimed and ran up the stairs to get ready.

He was back in a flash. Dad and Charlie were already sitting at the table. They were pointing at places on a map of the vast ranch. Joshua now knew why they had to have a map: the ranch was huge.

"Dad," he interrupted, "are we really going today?"

Dad turned away from the map and gave Joshua his daily "good-morning" hug.

"A promise is a promise," Dad said as he looked into Joshua's gleaming eyes.

3

"Awesome!" cried the boy. The startled cook whirled and chuckled as Joshua jumped up and down.

"A good trip requires a good breakfast," Dad said. "Let's sit down and give thanks for this food and for Mrs. Wooster's talent and heart for us."

Joshua normally loved breakfast. But he could hardly eat fast enough. He remembered his dream about running the horses alongside his dad. He kept thinking of the tent, the stars, the night air, and the lute his father made for him.

He hardly paid attention to the adults' conversation about campsites. His mind was already on the trails. His imagination was already thinking about occupying his dad's complete attention.

Before long, he found himself hugging Charlie, Mrs. Wooster, and the other servants in front of the barn. They surprised him with their ranch's peppy version of "Happy Birthday" as he and his father's horses trotted away.

"I know we're only going on a camping trip," Joshua said, "but I'm going to miss everyone."

"I know exactly what you mean," his dad said as he threw his hand out toward Joshua and received his customary "high-five" from his son.

The voices of the birthday singers trailed off as Dad and Joshua quickened the pace. Suddenly, Joshua felt the silence of separation. It was as if he and Dad had walked through a door and were now together in a different place. There were no ranch hands or cooks. Joshua listened as the birds picked up where the ranchhands' chorus left off. Their songs were persistent, varied, beautiful and loud.

Dad coaxed Joshua's horse along by speeding up. All of a sudden, Joshua could feel the cool wind against his face and he again remembered the dream. The ranch was just behind them, but he felt like he was in another world.

"Keeping up?" his dad asked.

"Tryin'" Joshua replied.

They were now on a long, straight trail that ran alongside a river as clear as crystal. Joshua had been on this one before. However, he'd never gone too much farther because Dad would always turn them around in time for lunch or dinner. He and his father had picnics there under some of the fruit trees that lined both sides of the river.

The water was so clean that Joshua could see the bottom where the schools of fish and the beauty of the rocks would steal his attention, and his eyes would stray from the path. Fortunately, Freedom had a loyalty in him to protect his master at all costs and so the horse allowed Joshua the liberty of day-dreaming.

If the river wasn't distracting enough, the unique single line of fruit trees would steal any rider's attention.

"Why did you plant the trees in a single row along the river?" Joshua asked. "With all this land, you could have made an orchard."

"Well, that was just the point," Dad raised his voice over the sound of the clomping hoofs. "With all this land, there's no need to plant the trees so tight together. This way, you can ride and pick the fruit. I like things simple."

Always thinking of other people, Joshua thought to himself.

As they continued, Joshua was impressed that his dad had alternated the fruit trees so that anyone could have a choice no matter where they found themselves on the path.

"How many types of fruit trees did you plant?" Joshua asked.

"Twelve," Dad replied. "One for each of your birthdays."

"No way!"

"Well, I actually planned one type for each month."

"Wow!" Joshua said.

Dad knew what Joshua was thinking, so he asked first.

"Would you like to stop talking about the fruit and start eating some?"

"That's just what I was thinking!"

They rode over to an apple tree.

"Can I climb it?"

"Sure, Joshua, just don't go to far out on the limb. Try getting us a couple from the top where the sun really ripens them."

When he reached the top, Joshua threw one down.

"Good catch, Dad." Joshua said. "This one tastes better than any I've ever tried before."

"That's the way good fruit tastes," Dad said. "It just keeps getting more delicious."

Dad not only enjoyed talking with his son, he loved watching him. He lay down under the tree eating his apple, looking up at his son who was perched at the top of tree. Joshua's dark brown hair was being blown by a gentle breeze, and there was a satisfied look on his face that made all of Dad's hard work on the ranch worth it.

The apple was just the right food for a snack. They stayed there for some time.

"It's a nice view of the river from up here," Joshua said. "I can see where we are going."

"Time to go before a cloud comes and takes you away with it," Dad said as he stretched a bit. "Besides, we've got to save some room for the pears down the road."

While the fruit would provide great snacks, Dad had prepared enough provisions for them to have a three-day camping trip. They could run the horses long and hard and not have to worry about getting back by sunset. He knew they could take breaks when they wanted, snack when they got hungry, or just ride along and enjoy each other's company.

The latter was Joshua's favorite. For Joshua, the best feeling in the world was just being beside Dad. But being next to his dad on a horse was even better. He would ask Dad a lot of questions. He always wanted to know how Dad felt about things. Joshua would ask him about the past and about the ranch hands. But they rarely talked about things beyond the ranch's borders. The ranch seemed so big, it was Joshua's entire world.

Later on, they slowed the horses down, and Dad asked if Joshua would like a break.

"Sure," Joshua replied. "Dad, is this the farthest you and I have ridden together?"

"I believe it is," said Dad. "But today is just the beginning. We'll head out through the deep forest tonight and set up camp there. Then we'll head out to the cliff on your birthday."

Joshua's heart leapt when his dad mentioned the cliff. He had seen it on the ranch map and had heard Charlie and Dad talk about it this morning. *What will I see?* he wondered.

Dad seemed to read his mind. With just a glance, his dad quizzed him.

"You're thinking about your trip to the cliff," Dad said. "I'll just say that it's a beautiful view. We can see the sunset and the sunrise from two vantage points. You'll love it. But I don't want to tell you too much beforehand because first impressions are best seen through your own eyes."

Joshua didn't exactly know what his father meant. But he trusted that Dad wasn't being secretive, just cautious. At times like this, Joshua could continue prying, and his dad wouldn't mind. But he had developed such a trust in him that he held off further questioning. Dad had never broken his trust with him yet. Besides, Dad liked surprises and his son took right after him.

"O.K." said Joshua. "I see it's time to change the subject."

His dad winked. "Next question."

"How do you ride so effortlessly for so long?"

"First of all, if I do, you're a chip off the old block because you rode well this morning."

"Graçias!"

"De nada," replied Dad. "Seriously, you really do."

"I keep a close eye on you."

"And I, you," said Dad. "I think a lot of life's mystery is solved right there."

"By looking at each other?" asked Joshua. "Well, actually, I kinda' know what you mean. There's something about 'bouncing off each other.'"

"You got it," Dad said. "Some call it synchronicity. Anyway, I've been riding for such a long time that I get to know my animal and my animal gets to know me."

"Synchronicity!" Joshua said.

"Yup," Dad said. "Sort of like when you and I sit in front of the fire and don't say too much but get a sense of what the other is feeling. Or like when you help me with the horses in the barn and you pull out a brush or a sponge before I even ask for it. That's how it is when I ride Starlight. One little tug or loosening up of the reins seems to do the trick."

"Like talking without talking."

"Sure," said Dad. "That's why it appears as if I'm riding effortlessly. You're handling Freedom the same way. In fact, I'm enjoying watching the two of you work together."

"Dad, which trail are we taking from here?"

"The one that goes alongside the forest. It turns right into the woods a few miles up. It's a smooth ride and cool. I think Starlight and Freedom will appreciate it as much as you and me."

"A few miles?" Joshua asked. "Just how far does our ranch go?"

"Too far to bother counting," Dad said as he smiled.

It was another of those many questions that Joshua left up to trusting Dad.

They mounted and made their way to the forest. The coolness felt great on the back of Joshua's neck. Hours later, as the sun began to lose its hold on the day, they stopped to set up camp. There was a wide circle in the center of the woods filled with the ashes from many old campfires now long gone cold.

Dad brought them to the center of the circle. After caring for Starlight and Freedom, the two built a fire as the sun went down. A slight chill descended upon the forest as the bird's songs seemed to wind down. Some owls picked up where they left off.

Before long, Dad's frying pan was sizzling with a stir fry mixture of some of the ranch's vegetables. As was his custom, Joshua paused before their meal and gave thanks to his father for preparing the meal.

Joshua was tired from the full day of riding and the heat. But the coolness of the evening kept him awake long enough to ask his father more questions about his first love: people. It was becoming a shared joy.

"Dad, how do you get to the point where you always think about others?" Joshua asked. "I mean, it's easier to think about yourself. Like just now, you had to be tired from the ride. Yet, you took care of the horses and then cooked me dinner. Not just any dinner—a delicious one. And the way you take care of the horses is the way you watch out for me. Do your needs just disappear because you're doing something for someone else? You just don't seem to struggle in your giving."

"Joshua, you're doing well just to perceive this," Dad said. "When something becomes a joy, it remains a task but it's pleasurable to perform. Cooking this meal was fun despite my weariness. Each time I prepare food, I'm looking for a slightly different way of doing it; to improve it somehow. I'm also thinking about the delight in your eyes, and hopefully in your stomach. The joy of serving just grows. It's like a field that rejoices to yield its crop.

"Joshua, there's a joy that springs forth from another's joy. Weariness or no weariness, the joy is mine, and I can see it growing in you. Speaking of weariness, son, I can see you're tired."

"I love you, Dad," Joshua said as he let out a yawn. He gave his father a kiss on the cheek and settled into his blankets. As he looked up, he saw the stars that must have inspired his dad when he painted the ones in Joshua's bedroom. Before he closed his sleepy eyes, his mind drifted back to his dad's words, "Joy grows." First, the stars in his bedroom. Now, the stars at the far end of the ranch. What was it about the stars? Why did Dad call his horse Starlight? What depth there was in the sky! What depth there was in his dad!

Joshua's senses stirred him. His ears overheard the birds heralding in the new day. His nose sniffed the eggs in Dad's fry pan, and his skin felt the dampness of an early morning in the woods.

"You slept soundly," Dad said, noticing his son's wakeful state. "Good thing, because we have a big day today." His father kept the conversation short to give his son time to dust the cobwebs off his consciousness.

After breakfast, Joshua spent time with Freedom. He wanted Freedom to know how much he appreciated him for his service and loyalty. The horse responded with some affectionate nudges.

The sun was well above the horizon as they made their way through the forest. Dad had purposely kept them in the woods for as long as possible to take advantage of its shade. They ate lunch under wisteria vines that provided a perfect ambiance of shade and fragrance. Joshua loved the violet-colored plant and all the bees it seemed to attract.

A while later, Joshua signaled his dad to slow down. By now, it was high noon and Joshua's thirst had gotten the best of him. He needed a break.

Dad slowed Starlight who seemed to like the idea of a stop. Dad steered them toward a low-lying tree.

"Ah," Joshua said, "what timing!"

It was a lemon tree.

"We'll cut one of these lemons and squeeze it into a cup of water," Dad said.

"This is perfect. It seems to revive you like a dip in the lake. Hey, Dad, do we have time for a swim? I bet Starlight and Freedom wouldn't mind," Joshua said.

"We do have to cross a river. It's flowing slowly right now so it will be safe. We'll take them right through."

Soon, they were doing just as Dad had said. This was nothing new for Starlight. Freedom, however, bucked a little as he settled into the water.

"I'd like to stay," said Dad, "but if we're going to get to the cliff for the sunset, we have to leave now. It's not that far."

Joshua now understood what his dad had meant about having a long ride ahead of them. With daylight closing down, Joshua knew they were close.

The campsite was in plain view, and Joshua could tell they were near the cliffs. No tree lines blocked their view, and the sky was beginning to paint itself a pale mauve that was subtly turning more pink.

Joshua's heart started beating quickly as he pulled up alongside his dad.

"It's beautiful!" Joshua exclaimed. "I've never seen anything like it."

"You haven't seen it all yet," Dad said, "Giddyup, Starlight!"

They made their way straight to the cliff, and it was everything that Joshua dreamed it would be and more. They sat close to each other, and even the horses seemed mesmerized by the sight. The sky was now glowing red.

Joshua felt Dad's arms around his shoulder, and it was as if they were attached at the heart.

"All I can say is, 'Thank you, Dad,'" said Joshua as he

tucked his head into his father's chest. "This is the most beautiful sunset I've ever seen. I could just stay here for the rest of my life. It can't get any better."

"Wel-l-l-l-ll," said Dad with a twinkle in his eye, "there's always the sunrise."

They basked in the beauty until the sun had dipped below the horizon and it was getting dark.

"It's time to set up camp, son," said Dad. They got up and, before long, Joshua was fast asleep close to his dad and the crackling campfire.

Whether it was the wind or a voice or someone in a dream that woke him, Joshua did not know. He only knew it was time to get up. It was still pitch dark and the campfire had almost died out completely. It offered only enough light for Joshua to notice the beginning of a trail. As if in a dream, he got up and seemed to watch himself walk down the path. On and on it went until the sky became a soft gray.

The trees were thinning out and the sky was becoming more prominent. He didn't know how long it had taken him to get there. Perhaps it had been a half an hour. Finally, the trail ended at another cliff.

Just as beautiful as the other, he thought. *Dad was right. I can't wait to see the sunrise.*

He perched himself on a boulder near the edge of the cliff. A large body of water shimmered in the dawn. Ever so slowly, a breach in the horizon turned golden yellow. Before long, the tip of the sun peered over the massive ocean. It streaked a path of gold across water directly to Joshua's spot.

"Oh, my!" Joshua kept saying to himself. "Oh, my!"

"Oh, my is right," said a voice behind him.

Joshua was startled. It was Dad. The hand was already on his shoulder to calm him.

"Have you ever seen anything like it?" his dad asked, already knowing the answer.

"Never," said Joshua. "Never."

Silence again as the two shared a mirror moment of last night.

"Dad," Joshua said, "I wish our ranch house could sit right on this cliff. It's an incredible site. Would you consider it?"

"I already have," Dad replied. "But I think it should be left alone. Some things just need to stay the way they are. To see the sunrise here is a view meant for all to see."

"I guess you're right," said Joshua as he stared and sighed over the water. "I guess you're right."

Joshua didn't know how long he had been there. He only knew that something inside was changing. Is this what was meant by coming of age? Was it just like the sunrise? A new day? A feeling had risen in his heart. What was it all about?

Back at the camp, Dad noticed Joshua's silence. He didn't say anything to his son. He knew better. He had to let Joshua process the stirring of his soul. Dad thought of all those who never noticed when their hearts were crying for their attention. They had deaf spiritual ears, numb hands, and blind eyes. But Joshua was not one of them. He was hearing, touching, and seeing. Dad would not interrupt the working of Joshua's senses.

In fact, Dad was pleased. It was like catching that sunrise. It was like seeing a leaf go from green to red, like seeing a wave from beginning to end, like understanding the wind. Dad treasured his son's metamorphosis. He would wait this one out. He would not interrupt.

Dad went about his usual business of closing up camp and preparing the horses while Joshua cleaned up and separated the ashes from the fire. It was time to leave, but Joshua didn't really want to go. It was the first time on the trip when he felt sluggish, torn between staying and going. How do you leave a place where the sun comes up every morning with orchestral awakening? Almost in a robotic manner, Joshua mounted his horse and followed close behind Starlight.

Still wondering what had happened, Joshua noticed that Dad hadn't spoken a word. He gave Freedom a gentle kick and the horse caught up to Starlight.

"Dad, I noticed we both got quiet back there," Joshua said. "There is something about beauty and depth that makes you want to burst. I can contain it, but I don't really want to. I feel exhilarated and lonely at the same time. I, I…"

"I know what you mean, son," Dad said. "But there's more to this trip. There is much more of the ranch's property to see and more for you to experience. We can't sit in just one room of the house or we won't get a feel for what is called a 'home.'"

"You're right, Dad," Joshua said. "But there was something about that particular spot. It's like a part in a book that you keep going back to and thinking about. Only I'm not sure I want to keep reading."

"Son," said Dad sternly, "I know you, and I know you want to keep reading. The best part of the book is always that which hasn't been read yet. And the best book you'll ever write is the one you're working on now. That's how this ranch is—it's full of surprises and wonders. You can never guess what that sunrise means each day. That is its real beauty. It's like the calling card of life that says, 'I'm here to do business.'"

"You have a way of making intensity make sense, Dad."

His father laughed.

Whatever his dad had just said seemed to snap Joshua out of his wonderment. He felt like he was back on the camping trip.

The cool of the morning gave way to a mid-day heat that made Joshua thirsty. They headed out of the woods and back to the riverside trail.

"Can we stop and get a drink?" Joshua asked.

"Sure, I was just thinking the same thing."

That was not the first time they would think alike.

Joshua scooped the water with his hands and almost intentionally let it run over his chin and down his neck to his chest.

"Oh," Joshua said, "that feels great!"

"In you or on you?" Dad joked.

"Water was made for both," Joshua said.

That gave him an idea. He started walking in.

"Joshua," cried his dad, "don't go in!"

The urgency in his dad's voice challenged his desires for a swim. He stopped in his tracks, but it was too late. The rock that Joshua stepped on was not secure enough and the current stole his footing. In an instant, Joshua's head was bleeding from another rock where he had fallen before being pushed downstream a short way until he became wedged between two large boulders.

Dad was there in a flash. Pulling Joshua out was a struggle. But the strong rancher hoisted his son onto his shoulders and fought his way to the bank. He ripped his shirt and proceeded to bandage Joshua's head.

With the care that only a father could show, he reached in his pocket and pulled out a vial of oil and anointed his son's forehead. Joshua's brown eyes slowly opened and their gaze said what words could not. A hug that seemed forever followed.

"I love you, Dad. I tried to stop but it was too late," Joshua said.

"The current isn't like back at the ranch house," Dad said. "It's swift and dangerous...very dangerous."

"I didn't know, Dad," Joshua said in an apologetic tone. "I should have asked you."

"That's O.K., Joshua," Dad said. "You couldn't have known. You've never been this far down river. Now you know. Anyway, it is tempting, but the water is flowing downhill slightly and it picks up speed and gets pretty rough here. Let's go up on the bank for a better view and some lunch."

"Dad, what's with the oil? It smells great," Joshua said.

"I've grown olives and herbs on the far side of the ranch and blended them. I call it 'The Oil of Joy' because it gave me so much joy to produce it."

"All I know is that it strengthened me immediately," Joshua replied.

"Joy and strength go together, son."

After Dad had washed Joshua's head, there wasn't even a cut to be seen.

Under a pear tree, they enjoyed lunch, and the pears were the best desserts Joshua had ever tasted.

Joshua's full belly and the heat combined to make him feel lazy. Dad didn't mind. He would catch forty winks, too.

There weren't many times when Joshua didn't dream dreams that sparked his imagination. This nap turned out to be no different. In his dream, he was in a waterfall and its roar was like nothing he'd ever heard. Under it, he could hardly keep his footing. Finally, he succumbed to its power and was swept under with a force he could not withstand. Water choked him as he went under.

He awoke in a sweat. Dad was there in a heartbeat.

"Are you all right, son? You must have had a bad dream."

Joshua just stared as if he was still in the dream.

"What is it, son?"

"There's a waterfall around here," blurted Joshua. "I can hear it. Dad, is there a waterfall around here?"

Dad's surprised look answered Joshua's question.

"Yes, son, there is," Dad said. "I was just going to take you there. We don't have to go if you don't want to."

Joshua was snapping out of it.

"No, that's O.K. We can go. I just had a dream that I got swept under a waterfall and it wasn't pleasant," Joshua said.

Dad put his arm around him and it seemed to reassure Joshua. Now he could clearly hear the sound in the distance. He wondered if that was what caused the dream or was it the morning's close call?

Joshua's dreams were more than thoughts staged out by his dormant mind. They were always significant. He felt uneasy as

16

he and Dad mounted their horses. The drone of the waterfall was intensifying as they rode. Suddenly, the two found themselves shouting to one another just to be heard.

Joshua forgot his dream in the excitement of the waterfall's presence. They couldn't see it yet, but they could hear it like it was next to them. Lush bushes and palm trees seemed to be protecting the falls like a fence.

But Dad knew just where he was going, and Joshua followed him through a slight opening in the greenery. A descending and winding path, which reminded Joshua of a jungle, led them to an opening adjacent to the river.

"I see why you didn't want me taking a swim," said Joshua. "I had no idea just how swift the current was. Dad, this is beautiful. I've never seen anything like it. Is there a campsite near here?"

"Right this way," said Dad as he kept his pace.

With every increasing decibel, Joshua's blood flowed accordingly. He was right behind Dad's every step. Dad slowed and signaled for Joshua to do the same.

"Son, we're very close to the edge," he warned. "Stay close and watch yourself."

The same kind of sternness that his dad expressed back at the river was in his father's voice again. There could be no mistakes. Just then, Dad came to a stop.

"Oh!" exclaimed Joshua. He started smiling, then laughed, and then yelled.

"Whoopee!" Joshua shouted. "Yeaahhhh!"

Dad laughed and high-fived him.

"This is worth the trip, huh?" Dad asked.

"Wow!" said Joshua. "Who would believe it? You have to see it to believe it!"

The cascading waterfall dropped water 800 feet down, and there was nothing like it in the world.

The river which ran from past the ranch to here was clear, rushing, cold, and majestic. What an ending to the trail!

They looked at each other again and sat on boulder. What else could they do but sit and take it in?

"You're right, son," said Dad. "There's nothing like it."

"Every stop just seems to get better," Joshua said. "This is the greatest birthday present ever!"

"My pleasure," said Dad. And he meant it.

"Where does all this water come from without coming to an end?"

"Love," Dad answered.

"What was that?" Joshua asked.

"It comes from love," Dad said. "That's where the river begins and ends. Water doesn't end because love started it, and love is inexhaustible. It sounds unbelievable, but it's true."

"Wow!" Joshua said. "Water comes from love, and rivers come from water, and this waterfall never ceases to display its founder."

"That sounds like a song," said Dad as he pulled his lute out of his backpack.

"Water comes from love and rivers from the water above..."

And then the song flowed like the liquid that had inspired it: "Water comes from love, rivers from the water above, through every rapid and bend, it sings the song that its Lover sends, and this waterfall roars in rounds and never ceases to display its Founder."

Over and over again, they sang along with the waterfall in three-part harmony until they could sing no more, and the waterfall took over from there.

The song was still in the air as they lay down for the night. The sound of the waterfall was not diminished, but it had become the norm. And in the shadow of its voice, Dad and Joshua heard nothing but its song in the night until it wooed them to a peaceful third night's sleep.

CHAPTER TWO

The dampness on their blankets was not so much dew as mist from the falls. But after the heat of the last two days, the coolness felt wonderful. A great fog had descended, making it quite dangerous near the edge of the cliff.

"Better start a fire and cook some breakfast and stay put," Dad suggested. "We're too close for comfort to walk around until after the fog lifts."

Breakfast never sounded constraining to Joshua, so he gladly helped his dad prepare some fish saved from the day before. The aroma of the breakfast mixed with the morning air seemed to say… "Happy Birthday!"

It was Joshua's 12th birthday, and he felt like quite the young man.

"Happy Birthday," exclaimed Dad after they had given thanks for the food.

"I almost forgot," said Joshua.

"Oh, come on," Dad teased.

"I said 'almost forgot,'" said Joshua.

"Well, now that you are a young man, what are you going to do as you get older," Dad asked.

Joshua paused. It seemed to divide their conversation in half. Like this birthday, it was like a new birth. He thought some more.

"I've always just wanted to do just what you do," Joshua replied. "I see the way you work; so hard. Most of what you do seems to be organizing, planning, and talking with people. It seems like so much."

"What do you mean?" probed Dad.

"Like that map, for instance," Joshua said. "The one that you and Charlie were studying of the ranch. It seems like the ranch is so big. I just don't understand how you keep up with everything."

"It's a lot like the waterfall. You asked where the water comes from. Everything has a source. I guess I just love people. I love to put them to work so they can use their talents to bring pleasure to others and themselves."

"Like Mrs. Wooster?" Joshua asked.

"Sure," Dad replied. "Why, she makes the best pancakes around. They aren't too spongy but have some substance. She always throws in some bananas or blueberries or who-knows-what in there for a special treat. They call that "panache." It's when a person goes beyond just doing what they have to do. They do it with pleasure and flare and, no matter how tired or bored, they know that what they're doing is the best thing they could be doing.

"Well, look at you," Dad continued. "When you were young, you would take care of Starlight and Freedom and the other horses. It wasn't some boring chore for you to work your way through. You had a relationship with them, and they responded. That's how I like to do things. Put my love into it and do it right."

"Anyway," Joshua replied, "I'd like to follow in your footsteps."

"Like father, like son," they said in unison and laughed at their timing.

"But you know, Joshua, you can follow in my footsteps exactly and still not do the exact things I do," Dad said.

"How could I do that?" Joshua asked.

20

"For example," Dad said, "we might have the same heart and mannerisms and yet it works its way out differently."

"I see what you mean," Joshua said. "I guess I'll know when the time comes."

"That's right, son. You'll know."

The morning seemed like a birthday; the kind of day that was made for the birthday person alone; the one date of the year when others deferred to him. Even the fog had pulled back its veil to open what would become one of the most memorable days of Joshua's life.

Heading back up the trail, Joshua and Dad took one more look from the higher perspective and stood in awe of the waterfall's magnificent drop. Straining to see to the very bottom, through the mist, Joshua could see some large boulders and swirling and crashing water. Its intensity triggered a remembrance of his waterfall dream from the day before, but he quickly and deliberately put it out of his mind. Dad knew by Joshua's look that something was bothering him, but he said nothing to his son.

It was another hot one. Dad went back up the trail with Starlight leading the way. They were riding up the river trail, but the river was flowing down, and it puzzled Joshua.

He signaled his dad to slow down.

"Are we headed home?" asked Joshua. "We seem to be heading against the river."

"Well, it's your birthday," Dad said with a gleam in his eye. "So, we still have some special moments ahead. Stay with me, son."

Dad and Starlight bolted with Joshua and Freedom right on their tail. About 20 minutes later, Dad slowed down to a trot and pointed straight ahead.

Joshua couldn't believe his eyes. Here, in the middle of nowhere, was a beautiful arching wooden bridge with side rails.

"Wow, Dad!" said Joshua. "Did you build that?"

"Not alone," said Dad. "Remember I told you I like to put people to work. Charlie and some of the men helped and we put this up in time for our camping trip. That's part of their birthday present to you."

Joshua just stared as they got closer. It was beautiful. The wood still smelled freshly cut.

A tear made its way down Joshua's cheek. Dad took notice, but said nothing. Joshua's emotions had been stirred by the large nameplate across the bridge's entrance, "Joshua's Bridge."

"Oh, Dad," his son said, "this trip just keeps getting better. I can't believe it. I can't believe it."

"It seemed appropriate," Dad said. "It's the perfect time and place to build a bridge."

"Why here?" Joshua asked.

"Let's ride across it, and you'll see," Dad said.

The wonderment in Joshua's expressions was worth all the work Dad had put into the planning and building of the bridge. Joshua was crossing more than a bridge. With Freedom's every hoofbeat, Dad could sense that Joshua was on the verge of young adulthood.

Joshua looked down over the raging river. He thought about what his dad had just told him about the other men helping him construct the bridge.

All this for me, he thought. *What's at the end of this bridge? Why here? Why me?*

He and his father came to the end of the bridge, and there was nothing but flat land in front of them and no tree line.

"O.K., Dad," he said, "What's next? I can't even imagine."

"Son," he replied, "you've seen a lot of beauty. And I have, too. In you, that is. I just suspect I'm going to see some more of that in you and that's why I brought you to the cliffs."

"Are these the cliffs that you and Charlie talk about?" Joshua asked.

"One and the same," said Dad.

They continued to ride straight ahead in perfect stride.

"After the sunrise, sunset, and waterfall," said Joshua, "I can't guess what could be more beautiful...ugh!"

Joshua squinted in disbelief and slowed Freedom to a trot. He didn't dare look at Dad because he didn't want his father to feel his disappointment. He stared and stared some more.

Black soot was rising up from beyond the cliff. It smelled and ruined everything about the scenic day.

"What is it, Dad?" asked Joshua looking for some explanation. "It's horrible."

They pulled their horses to a stop as they closed in on the edge of the cliff.

"It's pollution," Dad said. "From within a dirty soul comes foul air, foul everything."

Joshua didn't reply. The dad-trust factor kicked in. He went back in his mind to just a few minutes ago. Riding proudly along the river with his dad, sensing his destiny crossing the bridge. The majestic waterfall and now...this.

Father and son dismounted.

He stared at the site below. Smokestacks were billowing black air. Buildings and houses were nudged between the sea and cliff. Torches protruding from every corner. The sun's rays were blocked from its streets as the shadow from the cliff seemed to swallow up any hope for natural light. The sea appeared gray instead of the aqua from the other cliff. Bustling people were everywhere. There was activity on every alley. Voices were faint, but not at peace. The loudest sound was that of repetitive coughing.

"Dad, the ranch," he said almost begging for an explanation. "Dad, the ranch is perfect. Its homey-ness, the fresh air, the people, the love. Why couldn't they be like the people on the ranch?"

Dad sighed and finally released a word.

"Enemies," said Dad.

"Who would want to be an enemy to you, Dad?" Joshua exclaimed. "You're the best, Dad. Look what they have. For all this city's complications...they have nothing. And look at the ranch."

"Hate blinds," Dad said.

"Oh, Dad," Joshua cried. "Why?"

He sank to the cliff's edge and wept and wept.

It seemed like time stood still. Joshua didn't know how long he was there. But his dad's arms were around him and so nothing else mattered. As long as he was close, this nightmare could be withstood. Emotionally exhausted from the sight, Joshua continued to say nothing. Dad let him take it in.

Finally, Joshua lifted his head and opened his eyes as if to say, "I will not be defeated, and my dad will not be defeated, no matter the number of foes."

He felt stronger and cried no more. He turned to gaze on each part of the city. He would not look away. The birthday fireside conversation about his future flooded his mind.

"Now that you are a young man," Dad had said, "what are you going to do as you get older?"

"Dad," Joshua said in a determined voice, "I want you to grant me a birthday wish."

"Son," Dad said, "I know you well enough to say, 'Yes,' with no strings attached."

Joshua's eyes were red but they breathed life and excitement. He looked into his dad's eyes.

"Dad," Joshua said, "I want to have a birthday party."

Dad knew there was more to the request.

"Go on," Dad said.

"I want to invite these townspeople to my 13th birthday up at the ranch," Joshua blurted out. "We could pull out all the stops. Mrs. Wooster could be in charge of the banquet and Charlie could put up some extra houses. What do you say?"

"I say, 'No strings attached,'" said Dad.

Joshua hugged him with so much enthusiasm that he knocked Dad on his back, and the two hugged on the edge of the cliff.

"Like father, like son," said Dad as he lifted Joshua.

After taking the horses back to the water's edge for drink, they made their way back to the cliff and had lunch.

"Tell me about this city," said Joshua.

"It's called 'Northcliff,'" said Dad. "It faces the north and gets very little light because of the cliff. The inhabitants, for the most part, think that's normal."

"Dad," Joshua said directly, "I know you to be a generous man. I'm sure you've offered some alternative to these people. Right?"

"Yes, son," Dad said.

For the first time in a long time, Joshua saw a downcast countenance in his father.

"Yes, I did offer assistance more than once," Dad explained. "I offered various forms of aid ranging from helping them move the whole city to importing fresh produce here that we grow down on the ranch. The residents could never grow the fruits and vegetables you and I take for granted. They have to make a green mixture of bark and seaweed that they cook continuously. While they are very creative cooks, they don't have the ingredients that Mrs. Wooster does."

Pointing to the inmost crevice of the cliff, Dad continued.

"See that ice. Here we are in the heat, and they're down there having to use fires to warm their houses. You can see there are very few trees and so they have to use coal that pollutes their air. The cliff traps the cold air from the north wind, and it's like this all the time.

"It never lifts," Dad said. "They're trapped by their world: the cliff, the northwind and the sea."

"And a good deal of stubbornness if they turned down a man like you," Joshua interrupted. "It's hard to understand people like that."

"You'll understand them a lot better as you start passing out those invitations," Dad said. "Anyway, I met with the townsfathers and talked to them about options. They are an interesting bunch. It's hard to get a message past them to the people. They tend to have the admiration of the townsfolk. So, the people look to them for guidance on matters of planning, philosophy and the like. I'm not saying any of this to discourage you, son. Remember what we were saying about different roles? I think you were made just for this purpose."

"I'm just crazy enough to try it is what you really mean," Joshua jibed.

"No, I mean it," Dad replied. "You have a way of disarming people. Joshua, you are so sincere and loving, and, at your age…they won't be able to resist."

The two sat talking about Northcliff, the townsfathers, the townsfolk, and other assorted factors that Dad thought would come in handy on Joshua's trip. They sat there for a few hours; about as long as they could take the air.

"Son, we put in a direct road back to the ranch," said Dad. "It cuts right through the orchards, and at a good clip, we could make it back for dinner. What do you say?"

Joshua coughed and then smiled.

"I say, 'Which way is the trail?'"

In a matter of moments, they were riding quickly but precisely through a few bends and then onto the shortcut. The contrast of the beauty of the orchards with the streets of Northcliff played with Joshua's mind. It had happened so fast. His thoughts raced as fast as his horse as he began to envision the townspeople and their reactions. He began to plan provisions—the most irresistible representations of his dad's land and culture.

"They won't be able to resist," Joshua thought of his father's words as he looked over to his Dad and now applied that expression to him.

"I can't believe how far we've come so quickly," Joshua said. "I remember that spot over near the river."

"Won't be long now, son," Dad said.

And it wasn't. The bridge to the Ranch's entrance from the back side came into view and Joshua knew he was home. But all of a sudden, it hit him. He would be leaving the ranch and Dad and all the people for a year. It set a lump in his throat.

CHAPTER THREE

The sight of Charlie's outstretched hand was familiar to Joshua except that up until now he had always been on Charlie's end, welcoming visitors. Now that same handshake was welcoming him.

"Well, happy birthday, young man," Charlie said in hearty tone. "We've missed the two of you. It's bad enough with one of you gone, but two is too much."

Joshua quickly shot his dad a look that did not escape Charlie's notice.

"What's going on?" Charlie asked Dad.

"How about we go over it a little later, Charlie," said Dad with a patient wink.

"Well, we're all waiting for the birthday boy…uh, I mean birthday man." And Charlie gave Joshua the biggest slap on the back that the young man could remember.

"Let me take Freedom and Starlight into the barn while you both freshen up," Charlie said. "I know, the front left hoof will need to be looked at." Charlie winked back at Dad.

The empty house made Joshua's heart sink a bit. He was hoping to have a big reunion with Mrs. Wooster and some of the other help but there was not a soul in sight.

After washing up, Joshua laid down for a nap. The next thing he knew Dad was knocking on his bedroom door.

"Come on, Joshua," said Dad gently. "It's time for supper."

Joshua slowly lifted himself up, splashed some water on his face from his basin, and nearly bumped into Dad in the hallway.

"You first," Dad said pointing to the staircase.

Still a bit sleepy and even somewhat dreamy from his dream-like day, Joshua walked down the stairs into the family room.

"Surprise!" yelled half the help of the ranch.

Trying to disguise his sleepy frame of mind, Joshua happily received hugs from all over.

Some of the servants' children were eager to hear about Joshua's trip and gathered around him on the floor. He told them all about the camping sites, but he mostly enjoyed talking about having Dad all to himself, and the things he learned from their conversations and their riding.

"You made it all that way in three days!" exclaimed Sherra, an imaginative nine-year old who greatly admired Joshua. "You must have flown like the wind."

They all laughed at her expression.

"I'm telling you," Joshua said, "he's the best riding teacher you could ever want. All you have to do is be creative enough to keep your eyes on the path and him at the same time."

More laughter. They sat there and listened about camping in the woods, the sunset and sunrise, the close call at the river, Dad's healing oils, the river, and the waterfall. But Joshua deliberately left out the waterfall dream and the view of Northcliff.

Meanwhile, Dad sipped his freshly-made apple cider, complimented some of Mrs. Wooster's staff on the job they did on the food, and made his way over to where the group of children was listening to his son.

He noticed the predicament Joshua was in, and he came to his rescue. Knowing, for example, that Joshua would miss his friends when he went away and they would miss him, not the least of who was Sherra, Dad cleared his throat and caught Joshua's attention.

"Excuse me for a minute, I'll be right back," said Joshua to his friends.

While Dad and Joshua made their way through the crowd to the privacy of the back hallway, it did not escape the notice of the servants that something was troubling their young master.

"Dad," Joshua said, "they're all together. Now would be as good a time as any to tell them because I want to get going. If I stick around too long, I might lose the nerve. Anyway, I might as well tell them. They're my friends. They have a right to know."

"I think you might break Sherra's little heart," Dad teased, "but I understand your thinking."

"It's all so sudden," Joshua paused.

"Life is a lot like that river," Dad said. "It has its mellow times, but sometimes the current carries you along pretty swiftly. You're in a 'rapids' flow at the moment."

"I guess so," said Joshua. "What about Northcliff, Dad? You mentioned our staff is mostly from Northcliff. What about the kids? Should they know? Would the parents want them to know?"

"The parents trust me and they'll trust you; go with the flow," Dad said as he tousled Joshua's black hair.

In a moment, Joshua was back on the floor sitting amidst his friends. Dad motioned to the parents to gather around, so most of them figured it had something to do with the view from the cliff. But Charlie and his construction team had guessed that Joshua had crossed his bridge.

"Well," Joshua began, "this is hard to say. So, my best way of saying anything is just to come right out and talk about it."

The sensitive spirits of the children were on edge. Some looked sad. Others hung on Joshua's every word. The parents were shoulder to shoulder and the birthday boy had their complete attention.

"You know about the camping trip now," said Joshua. "But I didn't tell you the result of the outing. All during the trip, I had

30

this feeling that I was on the verge of something; something more than just a birthday. It felt like being born all over again – like starting something new. I've never felt anything like it before.

"Dad even asked me about my future and what I was going to do now that I was getting older," Joshua continued. "I'll tell you what I told him: 'I want to be like my dad.' But I didn't know how that would work itself out. Dad said that I could be just like him without doing the exact same things he did. He told me that I could still have his character and yet be who I was meant to be. He said I am like a messenger.

"Well, after we left the waterfall, we crossed over a new bridge that Charlie and his crew constructed. I crossed over that bridge and we came to another cliff…"

Joshua choked on his words and his eyes filled with tears. One of the young girls handed him a tissue. He continued.

"Billowing black smoke was coming from the cliff," Joshua said as he again choked up.

Looking into the eyes of the children and their parents, he continued to tell them about Northcliff and the effect it had had on him.

The children began to sob and the parents one by one put arms around their children. Dad went over and sat on the floor next to his son, giving him encouraging hug to go on.

"So I asked Dad for a 13th birthday present," Joshua said.

"Aren't you getting a little ahead of yourself?" joked one of the servants trying to lighten up the atmosphere.

"Not really," Joshua said. "It will take a year to prepare for it. I asked him for a 13th birthday party."

"Barely gets over one and wants another," another joked. Everyone was starting to settle down for the news.

"Well, I'd like to ask all of you to be part of it," Joshua continued, now getting used to the ribbing.

He outlined what was on his heart.

"Does that mean you'll be leaving for a long time?" asked seven-year old Steven.

"I'll be gone for one year," Joshua said.

Each child took it a different way. Some were upset, some were resigned. But Joshua assured them that he would come back.

It had been a big night, and after all the questions were answered and the party was over, a spirit of exhaustion came over the whole place.

Lots of hugs and tentative looks came Joshua's way at the doorway of his house and heart.

Weary from the long day, he kissed Dad goodnight.

"That was the best birthday any son could want," Joshua said. "Thank you for being you. Thank you for all you do."

"Sounds like a song, son," Dad joked.

Joshua just waved off his dad. "Maybe another night," the weary boy said.

"I love you, son," Dad said. "Goodnight."

Another night, another dream.

Joshua couldn't make out the figure's face, but he was in a black overcoat and seemed to be bidding Joshua to come. Joshua approached cautiously down a slightly rocky decline. The footing was tricky.

Again, the figure waved him on. As Joshua got closer, the man held out his hand in a welcoming manner as if to help steady Joshua from the descent.

Joshua took the man's hand, whereby the man promptly laughed and strong-armed Joshua over his shoulder as if to throw him down the descent. The man's hand was cold and slippery, but Joshua would not let him go. The two clung together until finally Joshua could see the man's soot-covered face and dark eyes. Joshua held tightly and looked over his shoulder. He was on the ledge of a cliff.

Rousing himself, Joshua was hanging over the edge of the bed sopping wet and expected to see soot-covered hands. They were just cold with sweat. He stared at his bedroom floor. The early morning sun cast its welcoming and familiar yellow reflection on the wood of his night table. Nothing in his room had changed, but everything inside the 12 year-old was different. Lately it seemed he had to defend his life in nearly every dream.

"Can Northcliff really be this dark?" he asked himself, spinning back on his bed as if to redirect his posture away from the cliff. He wiped off his wet brow with his sheet.

"I will know you when I see you, and I'll know what to do," Joshua mumbled. "I saw your face. I'll know."

"Know what?" Dad asked from the doorway. "Who are you talking to?"

"Come on in, Dad," said Joshua, trying to compose himself.

"Is there someone under the bed?" Dad teased.

"Dad, you know better than to joke this early," Joshua said as he leaned up slightly to give Dad a hug.

"I'm sorry," said Dad. "Couldn't resist. Who were you talking to?"

"Dad," said Joshua, "what's with these dreams I'm having? Every time I turn around, I'm having nightmares. It seems like someone or something is after me. Do you think it's Northcliff, Dad? I never had these types of dreams before the camping trip."

"Slow down, son," Dad said as he stroked Joshua's wet hair. "Boy, are you wet! Something must have really scared you. Joshua, please tell me about the dream."

And Joshua obliged.

"Sounds like your spirit is preparing and warning you," Dad said. "I know you are smart enough to understand that taking on Northcliff is no small project. People will resist you, and you will have enemies. I'm glad you got a good look at your adversary in the dream. He's real. Just as you've described him. He's like a gatekeeper to the city. There's no way around him. He lives on the cliff on the only way down.

"But I don't want to scare you, Joshua," his dad continued. "You are up to this trip, gatekeeper or no gatekeeper. Everything you've learned on this ranch has prepared you for this journey. You go with my blessing. You go with my heart."

"Like father, like son," Joshua said, lightening the conversation and waking up a bit.

"Like father, like son," repeated Dad. "Anyway, Charlie and I were up pretty early and were talking. We had a sense that you wanted to get going soon...

"...before I change my mind?" Joshua sneaked in.

"No," Dad said confidently, "nothing like that. But when Joshua makes up his mind, it's like it's already done. Anyway, we got talking and Charlie brought out a big old wagon that he thought Freedom wouldn't mind pulling. You'll be able to bring a sampling of the ranch with you which, believe me, you will need. Even when they bite into what we have up here, there will be those with no tastebuds..."

"Or taste," Joshua joked.

"Or taste," said Dad. "So, you'll be able to take good fresh fruit and vegetables with you. In their culture, you may be looked at as backward. The town fathers tend to think of themselves as very sophisticated with their seaweed factories and the like. Some of the bodies of the people have become so used to their food that they may physically reject it. However, there are hungry people in Northcliff who will eat and be satisfied. They will understand what you are offering is not a fad or false hope. Charlie will fill your cart up with the best of the best, and you'll be off."

"How soon, Dad?" asked Joshua.

"As soon as you can talk Freedom into the idea of saying 'Goodbye' to the ranch for a year."

"He'll understand," Joshua said as he looked into his father's eyes. "He'll understand."

"And so do I, so do I," said Dad. "But we're going to miss our young man."

"And I'll miss you and everyone here," said Joshua. "I'll miss the sun. It's so dark there. But if I keep my mind on the party, I'll be able to take it. I know it's going to be different, Dad. I won't be able to come into your den at nights."

"I'll be with you in spirit, son," said Dad. "And I'll look forward to that party, too. Don't concern yourself about it. Charlie, Mrs. Wooster and some of the women and kids will take care of everything. It'll be a party to beat all parties. Tell your friends down there that there will be plenty of everything. We'll have places built within a year to house them permanently if they like it so much they want to stay here. And the same crew that built your bridge will be working on another surprise over there."

"I won't bug you about the surprise," Joshua said with a smile, "but as far as liking it up here, they won't be able to resist the love that you and the men will put into their housing and the party and the food. They'll love it! I can't wait to tell them…"

Joshua's voice trailed off just enough for Dad to notice.

"What is it, Joshua?" his Dad asked quickly.

"It's just that, well, I wonder, I mean living down there… I just wonder if they will believe me," Joshua said. "They may think I'm lying or exaggerating. Why would they believe me?"

"But what would be the point in lying?" Dad said. "Besides, you'll be well-stocked with fruit, vegetables, oils, clothes and other things. Just one taste of your water jug should convince them. Those with eyes will see. Joshua, I know you. You'll want everyone to come to your party, but everyone won't come. There will be those who think you just want attention and a lot of presents. Others will be afraid of what they'd have to leave behind. Still others will say they know me and that they have everything there that we have here. Yet, I know you'll want everyone to be here, and those who won't accept your invitation will hurt you. I wish I could go with you, but I see this is something that you have to do on your own."

"Speaking of invitations," Joshua said.

"We've got that covered," Dad said as looked straight into his son's eyes.

"I'll be counting the days until your 13th birthday, Joshua," Dad said and gave Joshua a hug that had a note of finality to it.

"I'll be counting, too," said Joshua. "I love you."

"Get dressed and let's go outside," said Dad. "We've got some company."

As they walked out unto the front porch, a cheer erupted. All of the sleepyheads from the night before had awoken and were running up to Joshua to get their last hugs in before his departure. Sherra handed an envelope to Joshua.

Choked up, Joshua sat on the steps and read the young girl's note: "You are invited to my friend Joshua's 13th party. It will be the most wonderful celebration. Please come."

One by one, the children handed Joshua their hand-made invitations. They all said roughly the same thing. Joshua was moved and kept shaking their hands, patting the little one's heads, and giving hugs.

The adults surrounded him next. Many handed him keepsakes from their homes to remember them by. Joshua's heart was full. Everything was happening so fast. Yet, everything felt so right.

His friends backed off a bit so that Joshua and Dad could have a last moment together. Helping Joshua up onto the cart, Dad gave Joshua his personal walking stick.

"Joshua," Dad said, "take good care of this stick. I use it every morning on my walks. It looks tame, but it's tip is sharp. It will come in handy for all sorts of occasions. You don't have to do much defending up here, but you never know down there."

Joshua noticed the intensity in Dad's eyes. It was Dad's way of warning without scaring. Their eyes filled and both necks seemed intertwined before Dad finally pulled back enough to suddenly see his son in a different light. Joshua's eyes were red, but his heart was stout. He seemed stronger and more robust than the boy before the camping trip.

"I'll keep it close," said Joshua. "It'll be like having a piece of you with me."

"You don't know how true that is," Dad said, holding his hand out for one last handshake.

After boarding the cart and driving a bit, he slowed down to look over his shoulder. He could see his dad's eyes glistening and others wiping their noses. His eyes again filled so completely that he could barely see where he was going.

The ranch was far behind now, and he finally lost sight of Dad. He stopped the cart and cried like a baby. Freedom turned a bit.

"It's O.K., Freedom," he sniffled. "Your master is fine."

He sat there a few more minutes trying to regain his composure.

"Giddyup" was all he could muster.

CHAPTER FOUR

D own the steep trail, Freedom listened to his "friend" while keeping up his pace.

"I hope you don't mind, Dad," he said to himself. "I just can't stop talking to you just because you are far away."

Freedom looked back to see if he picked up a passenger.

"Oh, Freedom," Joshua said, "it's just me talking to my dad. Somehow, I think he probably hears me. Well, I think you and I will have a lot of conversations as well. You're the best horse a boy could ever want."

Freedom seemed to respond to the compliment and brightened the pace.

"Whoa!" Joshua said. "Remember, we're going downhill, and I've never driven this wagon before."

Freedom obliged and they came to the hairpin curve that Dad had marked on the map. His father had been up most of the night preparing a progressive map and notes to put in Joshua's satchel.

Joshua could see down the mountain that the campsite was only a few miles ahead. He continued because he was tired and wanted to make it there before dusk.

His wagon was a covered one, and Charlie had fixed up a bed inside on a board on top of the provisions. But tonight was mild, so Joshua decided to sleep under the stars. The rice and beans were barely digested when he lay down beside the warmth of the fire. His eyes were playing tricks on him. He thought he saw Dad across the glow of the fire. He sat up, but it was just wishful thinking.

"Oh boy, Dad," Joshua said, "I'm gone one day and I'm already homesick. Only 364 more to go."

The closest thing he really had to Dad was the walking stick beside him. The beauty of the oak wood and the perfect shape with which Dad had whittled it caught his eye and his imagination at this weary moment. Reaching in his pocket, he pulled out a knife and carved "D.A.D." on the side of the cane.

"That's an acronym for 'Deliverance and Destiny,'" he said. "That's my dad."

Drowsy from the emotional day, he fell fast asleep. His rest was deep until the laughter woke him.

Freedom was stirring, and it was darker because the fire was all but out. He looked around.

Was it the gatekeeper? Was it an owl?

Joshua remembered his dad's word about respecting the gatekeeper's position without being afraid of him. In the distance, the voice again made Joshua shiver. It was deep and lacked discretion. The sound followed the same regularity as that of an animal in the night.

It was still the deep of the night and Joshua pictured Dad across that campfire.

"Go back to sleep, Joshua," the image seemed to say. "Go back to sleep."

And Joshua obeyed his half-awake senses as his Dad's voice overpowered the laughter.

"Goodnight, Dad," Joshua said as he dozed off again.

There was no scent of fish or oats or anything else when Joshua awoke. How he missed Dad. The chill of the morning inspired him to start a fire, boil some water, and give Freedom the attention he needed.

He was the responsible one now. Joshua knew how to get

going from watching his dad. Going about his chores, he sensed that he had crossed the line into young adulthood. There was no one else to rely on. He thought of the chores as a precursor to what lie ahead—especially with regard to the gatekeeper.

His dream about the dark figure from the night before was still fresh in his mind. Joshua's mind crept ahead. Wouldn't meeting up with the gatekeeper be the same as a chore? It was something that his dad had entrusted to him and had said he was capable of handling. By the time Joshua had cleaned up from his oatmeal and fresh apple breakfast, the matter was settled. He couldn't wait for his next birthday and yet he had to wait. He made up his mind to take each day as it came, no matter how slow or fast the day went. Today would be no different.

He would hitch Freedom and get going; laugh or no laugh, dream or no dream.

"Sssssss!"

Freedom was spooked by the sound of the snake. There were no snakes at the ranch, but Joshua reached for D.A.D. without thinking and speared the serpent before the creature had a chance to move. Freedom calmed down immediately.

"Wow!" Joshua yelped in relief. "That was monstrous!"

Freedom seemed to nod in agreement.

While he couldn't see over the edge of the cliff from his propped up seat, he sensed he was near it. As such, he held Freedom's reigns with caution, trusting his horse and yet protecting him as well.

Joshua never realized how long and how steep the mountain was before another sharp bend slowed Freedom down. Joshua picked up on a figure in the distance. This had to be the gatekeeper. He seemed innocent enough. But then Joshua remembered the dream of the hand that was meant to deceive.

He slowed down and looked to see if the gatekeeper had any "help" off the path. The man appeared to be alone.

"Welcome," said the gatekeeper.

Joshua slowed his buggy and studied the man. His dream was still registering a strong caution.

"Hello," Joshua said politely, but confidently.

"You're a spitting image of your father."

"Thank you," Joshua said.

"Care to rest for a while?"

"Don't mind if I do," Joshua said and promptly got down off the wagon. "My name is Joshua."

"People just call me 'Gatekeeper,'" he said, shaking Joshua's hand. "From years of service come nicknames."

"How many years?" Joshua asked as they sat by the man's gate and made themselves comfortable next to a fire.

"I don't even know how many years," he said.

The conversation proceeded politely before the gatekeeper introduced the subject of Joshua's destination.

"I'm visiting Northcliff for the first time," Joshua said.

"Planning to stay a while?" he asked, looking over at the sizable wagon.

"As a matter of fact, yes," Joshua said, not exactly volunteering information.

"Well, that's great," he said. "I've got quite a responsibility here and I could use some help. You're going to need food to live in Northcliff. The diet is quite different down there."

"Thank you for thinking of me," said Joshua, "but my father has set me up with enough provisions. He's given me all I need."

"Well, you're going to need friends," he said. "We have healers should you stumble, fall off a horse, or take in too much of the soot from Northcliff. You can't go this alone."

"My dad has given me oils for healing," Joshua replied. "He's set me up pretty well."

"Well, everyone needs to work," he said, motioning Joshua

to the edge of the cliff. "From here, you can see the entrance to the city gate. I am offering you a job, which believe me, is of incredible worth. There's not a lot of work to be had that's as pleasing as working for the Gatekeeper. We'll keep you on the posts away from the soot. Just say the word, and you can work for me. Someone with your ability shouldn't be working in the seaweed factories."

"I appreciate the offer, but…" Joshua said.

"But what?" he interrupted, his face growing red. "You've got to work or you won't survive. It's not as cushy as your ranch. You need me, and I'm willing to take you under my wings. You should reconsider. Not every one gets to work for the Gatekeeper."

"I'm sure you're right," Joshua said firmly, wishing his dad was there to take up the conversation from here. "But I've always worked for my dad and I think I always will."

"You're dad wouldn't be caught dead down in this polluted town," he replied. "How can you work for a rancher in a city? You're going to need me."

"Thanks for the cup of water," Joshua said. "But I've got to get going."

Gatekeeper hid his disturbed feelings as best he could, but Joshua knew the man was not pleased.

"You don't have permission to proceed," he said, looking at Joshua with an intimidating scowl. "I am the Gatekeeper, and I deny you passage."

"With all due respect, Gatekeeper," said Joshua just as sternly, "my dad owns this mountain, and I'm simply riding on his property. I don't know what jurisdiction you think you have, but check my dad's deed."

He pulled out the map that Dad had given him and pointed it out to the man.

"That's your dad's version of a map," he said, raising his voice. "You are denied passage."

42

Joshua put the map away, spoke to Freedom in a whisper, and gently undid the lever of the wagon's brake.

Gatekeeper pulled at the young man's arm with an overpowering tug. Joshua reached for Dad's stick behind the seat and quickly swiped the man's face.

Stricken from the blow, he swirled and hit his head against the post of the gate and fell. Blood was running down from the cut that ran from the forehead past his eye and over the top of his cheek.

Joshua ran to unlock the gate, jumped into the front seat, and Freedom took off. He looked over his shoulder to see the man rolling on the ground in severe pain.

"You'll pay for this!" he yelled. "You'll pay."

His voice faded under the hoofbeats and the rattling of the wagon. Freedom knew what he was doing: keeping his head while he managed the pace and protected his master from danger.

"Thadaboy!" he yelled. "Way to go, Freedom!"

Joshua's heart was racing. He had never seen such hatred and deception on the ranch.

"Come on, Freedom," Joshua said, "let's make tracks."

The horse complied, and they were traveling at a good speed that made the provisions in the wagon roll around. There would be time to straighten that out later. For now, he wanted to put some distance between himself and Gatekeeper.

"I'm sure the townsfathers will hear about this in no time," said Joshua. "Still, it's only another 364 days."

Freedom might not have appreciated the humor, but the comic relief calmed Joshua's nerves. He slowed his horse. By now, Joshua could smell the sea. It was so different from the dry air of the ranch's plateau. The water was in sight and still no sign of the polluted air. He wondered why the people didn't move out of Northcliff. What was it about Gatekeeper and the townsfathers that cast such a spell over the inhabitants?

It was obvious after that encounter that Gatekeeper wasn't stationed just to keep people out of Northcliff. He was sure it worked both ways. His "patrol" kept people from leaving too.

Joshua shivered from raw nerves mixed with the coolness of the water's breeze. The waves crashed with a force against the gigantic seaside boulders. Slowing Freedom down, he pulled up and let Freedom drink from the brook that was quickly flowing into the sea.

The "chore" of meeting Gatekeeper was done, although he was sure the "You'll pay" was a promise that the man was going to keep. He put this out of his mind, remembering that he had a long way to go before his 13th birthday party.

"It'll be worth it, Dad," he said aloud as Freedom turned again to see who he was addressing. Freedom was beginning to get used to such dialogue. "I can't wait to see you again. What pain this Gatekeeper must inflict on these people. Thanks for your stick. I sure learned to use it in a hurry... C'mon Freedom."

They were a few hundred feet above sea level and the sharp left bend left them on a road between a higher cliff and the water. For the first time, Joshua could see the soot. Going from the beauty of mountain's plateau into this was quite depressing. The thicker air seemed to cast a weight on his shoulders like no rainy day ever could.

CHAPTER FIVE

It was like passing through a veil between day and night; between a dream and a nightmare. It certainly wasn't the same as viewing it with his father from the plateau. Passing the sheer cliff on the left, Joshua realized there would be no turning back, no matter how depressing. He had just entered the geographic gate to the city.

Some brush could not hide the movement of a small creature to his left. A stone grazed the side of his head, but Joshua's spirit was steadfast. He ignored the sting and shock and kept Freedom at a steady pace as the road declined a little more. He eventually paused to view the path before him. Several hundred yards ahead and to the right was a small cabin exuding some soot with all its accompanying acrid odor. The oppression was so thick he could cut it with a knife. No more noise came from the brush.

He couldn't help but notice that it was suddenly dusk, although it shouldn't have been dark already. But he was on Northcliff time now, where the darkness captured the day. Joshua was starting to feel either the strain from the day or the oppression from his entrance to the town. Either way, it meant a visit to that cabin if only to satisfy his hunt for a suitable place to bed down his horse for the night.

As he and Freedom eyed the place, a little red-haired girl looked up from her task of washing some clothes in the stream alongside the house and stared at him. Her tangled hair covered most of her face. Her green eyes grew big with either fear or wonderment. She looked intently at Joshua and his horse.

"Who are you?" she asked with an accent.

Joshua pulled up and looked at her for just a second. His heart was stirred and the oppression that clouded his entry seemed to dissipate at once. A teardrop fell without a fight from his sleeve or hand. He cleared his throat.

"I'm Joshua and this is my best friend, Freedom," Joshua said, recovering from his emotional first impression.

"I'm Liza," she said in a funny tone. Joshua could just barely understand her.

He slowly dismounted and shook her hand. Her fingers were tiny and frail.

"I betcha' you're seven," Joshua said playfully.

"How did you know that?" Liza asked. "Do you know my mother?"

"No," Joshua said. "But I know kids!"

The girl laughed and showed some life beyond her guarded welcome. Her hair had hidden several marks all over her face. Joshua couldn't figure out whether they were from the polluted air, the dirt, or bugs. He tried not to stare to protect her dignity. She did not notice his inspection, however, as much as she noticed the cleanliness of his face and hair.

She liked Joshua. He seemed big, like an older brother. But he had a kind confidence that sparked her imagination and triggered one question after another. Finally, Joshua sensed it was time to meet her mom. He didn't think it wise for a mom to come upon a strange young man talking to her little girl.

"Sure, come on in," she said, abandoning her chore and taking Joshua's hand. They left Freedom to drink in the stream.

Liza had just met Joshua and already liked to be near him. Holding his hand made her feel like she owned something special, better than any toy, doll or imaginary friend.

Joshua just felt honored. He had hit paydirt on his first stop! It made him forget his fear that he had made some terrible mistake, that he wasn't up to the task of making a difference in Northcliff much less leaving home for a year. This Liza seemed to turn Joshua back into the Joshua of the ranch. She seemed like the real gatekeeper.

Joshua's heart melted as they entered the humble shed-like cabin. The seaweed smell almost overpowered him. He hid a slight cough with his hands.

Like the girl's facial marks, this odor was something that he would just have to get used to so as to not offend the residents.

The inside of the cabin was bright with colors. Crudely framed paintings of their immediate surroundings were on the walls. Joshua eyed them while Liza eyed him.

"My mommy and I are artists," she said.

"I can see," he said, emitting a slight cough again, "you're both very good."

A small, dark-haired woman stooped to make her way out of a tiny bedroom door.

She was surprised to see a visitor, but her daughter's confidence created a sense of ease.

"This is Joshua," Liza said. "He's my friend. Joshua, this is my mommy, Mrs. Aqua."

Joshua's heart was playing those funny tricks again. Looking into her eyes reminded him of being with his dad on the camping trip when they had sat and looked out over Northcliff for the first time. If it wasn't for Dad, he wouldn't be in this woman's house. If it weren't for Dad, he wouldn't have this heart.

He cleared the lump in his throat and extended his hand.

"Liza is so charming," he said. "You must be so proud."

"She knows a friend when she finds one, that I can tell you," said the mother in the same accent. "And please, just call me 'Aqua'—everybody does."

After talking a bit, Joshua accepted her invitation for dinner.

"Would you like to meet my horse, Aqua?" asked Joshua. "He's the best."

After Joshua introduced the two, he took care of Freedom for the night and entered the cabin, ducking through its short and narrow entrance.

The seaweed food that Dad had spoken of was a mixture of some sort of flour and seaweed. It was gritty and salty which made Joshua thirsty. He braved his first meal while holding Liza's hand.

"So where does a fine young man like you come from?" asked Aqua. "We don't get many visitors."

"I'm from my dad's ranch just up the mountain on the plateau," Joshua answered. "It's a beautiful place."

Joshua kept chewing. There was an awkward silence and Aqua and Joshua both recognized the need for further details. It was a mistake to be coy, and it was an error Joshua wouldn't make again. He had come for a purpose, and there was no sense in subtleties in a home as warm as this one. But Joshua's approach would be his own; not some anti-Northcliff spiel. He would simply talk about those things and people whom he loved.

"You and Liza would love my dad," he said in an excited manner. "And he would love you."

He had their attention and Liza's eyes were as big as pancakes. They looked at Joshua with a hunger in their eyes that Joshua instantly noticed.

"Some people say Dad is a bigger version of me and others would tell you that I'm a younger version of him. Anyway, he's the most wonderful man you'd ever want to meet. He's tall, smiles genuinely, and is a great rider. He's the best rancher in the world. He oversees farming, orchards and grows beautiful flowers…"

Joshua paused. Images of his last few days flooded Joshua's mind: the excitement of the camping trip, the lemon tree, getting saved out of the rushing river, the stars, the campfire, the sunset and sunrise, the waterfall, the bridge and the view from the cliff.

His friends picked up on his delay.

"Tell us more," Liza said.

"What I'd really like to say about him the most is that he is kind," Joshua said with redness in his eyes.

Being sensitive artists, Liza and her mom were beginning to see the portrait of Dad in Joshua's vulnerable eyes. They had known what it was like to read eyes like one reads a book. It was part of the reason they were on the outskirts of Northcliff. They were outcasts. Their soft spirits made them an easy target of the townsfathers. But Joshua was unlike any young or old man that they had ever met.

"Please," said Aqua, "go on."

"It's so hard to express the love I have for this man," he said. "There is a kindness in his eyes that is like a magnet. You just get hooked, and he has your complete attention and loyalty. I've learned everything I know from him. There is nothing I do or say that hasn't been the result of watching him. When I was younger than Liza, he would strap me to his back and take me for long horse rides through the orchards. He taught me how to climb trees without snapping limbs. He taught me everything I know about fruit."

"What is fruit?" Liza asked.

Her mother looked toward Joshua. She had heard of it, but thought it better to let Joshua explain.

"Oh, I almost forgot dessert!" Joshua exclaimed.

"What's dessert?" Liza asked.

"Stay right here," Joshua said, abandoning his description of Dad in favor a demonstration of his goodness. He hurried back in the door with the most ripe pomegranate he could find.

"What is it?" Liza asked in her cute accent.

"It's a type of fruit," he said. "You're going to love it. A pomegranate."

"A what?" Aqua asked.

"It's a pom-e-gran-ate," Joshua said distinctly. "It's one of the tastiest and most fascinating fruits that Dad grows. When I was little, we'd sit under its tree after a long ride and just eat these until we were satisfied. The aroma of the fruit when it's fresh and the air and Dad's company are some of my best memories."

"Actually," Aqua said, "it sounds like you have a lot of good memories."

As she watched him rip into the fruit with enthusiasm, she was thinking that good memories were rare in Northcliff. Joshua seemed so radically different. It wasn't that he was strange. But her mind had to make adjustments to handle his lightness. Liza seemed to adjust easily. She just kept giggling as she watched juice drip over Joshua's leg and his animated reactions to it. He had a bit of a showman's knack when it came to children. He also had an intrinsic navigational skill to the center of their hearts and that road ran both ways.

Within minutes, they were sucking the sweetness out of every last seed and laughing as Liza spit the remnants into a bowl. The dessert was a hit and Joshua's mind savored the moment like the Aquas savored the pomegranate. A kinship kindled that night that took the chill out of his homesickness.

More stories kept Liza's sweet eyes barely open until her mother realized that they were being held up by Joshua's sheer charisma.

Joshua also picked up on it and suggested a lullaby. After returning from the cart with his lyre, he told Liza to sit in her mom's lap. He related how his dad would make up stories and songs at night, and how he would fall asleep thinking about them. Sometimes, these thoughts would turn into beautiful dreams. In the morning, his dad would playfully call him the "dreamer" and ask him about them.

Liza smiled and yawned at the same time.

Northcliff had music, but it was very precise; its beats were perfect and monotone. The words were usually provincial and inhibited by their ignorance of the outside world. So when Joshua began to sing sweetly and lightly about his new young friend, her wakefulness rebounded enough to hear his clever chorus.

"Pomegranates are sweet, but not as red as the cheeks of my precious Liza," he sang over and over to her delight until her eyes slowly closed and opened and closed and opened and closed and opened no more.

Aqua whispered, "Thank you. Please, Master Joshua, do not sleep in the cart. Stay here in the living room, and we will get another log for the fire."

Joshua felt at home and couldn't resist, seaweed odor or no seaweed.

"Thank you," he said. "I'll lie down right here after I say 'Goodnight' to Freedom."

And sleep he did. The confrontation with Gatekeeper and the day's travel did him in.

Aqua provided her guest with a modest floor mat and came back for one last look at him before she retired. She felt as if someone had dropped off a treasure chest in her house. After all the hurt and rejection she had been through, she could hardly believe love would visit her and bring the same kind of peace to her that he now felt in his own rest.

He squinted through the fire again at his dad.

"Dad," he said, "I've never felt anything like this before. I feel like they are long lost cousins or something. I was so concerned about leaving my house. But here I am in another home. I'm well supplied."

"But you need your rest, son," Dad seemed to reply, "now go to sleep."

The fire was smaller, and he could see past the flames. No dad, just a dream that sacredly connected the camp with this early hour experience.

"But it was so real," he said to himself. He had heard himself say that before.

"I miss you, Dad," he said, tucking the blanket under his chin. "But you were right in saying that you'd be here in spirit. I can feel you just as close as the many times I fell asleep in your den chair."

Joshua's bones were cold for the first time in his life. No reflection of the sun rose in this house. In fact, Northcliff had little sunlight. Embers were the remainder of last night's dream. He wanted to stay under his blanket, but he thought that Freedom might be cold too and that motivated him to drag himself off the floor.

He went straight to the cart, pulled out his woolen top and quickly put it over his head. Freedom was happy to see him.

"I'm sorry, buddy," Joshua said as he stroked his friend, "I had no idea how cold it gets down here."

Aqua noticed Joshua's absence and took a moment to contemplate the meaning of his visit. She was used to being alone and making do on her own. Now, this bright ray of sunshine walked into her life. Would he walk out like most of the men in Northcliff? What did he want? He said he had come from a ranch. He seemed too genuine to be sent secretly from the townsfathers to check up on her.

But what about "Liza's Lullaby" as he called it? Wasn't that giving false hope to a child who had been routinely ridiculed by other children because of her cracked and peeling cheeks. The Northcliff children seemed to have a contest as to who could make the most clever insults about Liza's face. Why would

Joshua choose to sing about the most vulnerable part of the girl's body? Was he trying to be nice or was he naïve? Perhaps boys don't realize what a skin condition means to a girl, and he was just innocent enough not to understand. Do males ever care about anything? Could he possibly be different? It was almost beyond her mental capacity to fathom a man who was sensitive to a female's needs. Not in Northcliff.

"Good morning," Joshua said in a soft tone, interrupting her intense emotional state. "I thank you for giving me a place to sleep. It was very kind of you."

If there was one thing Joshua could do, it was to read people like a book. Her troubled countenance was not masked by her polite greeting.

"Aqua," he asked sincerely, "have I done something to offend you? You really look as if something is bothering you."

She hesitated, caught between a desperation to take the young man at face value or succumb to her experience with other males. Somewhere between that polarity, Joshua had unknowingly forged his way into her trust, and she blurted out her concern about "Liza's Lullaby."

Joshua begged her forgiveness.

"You must believe me," he said, "I have no intentions to deceive. I seem to have an ability to see things that haven't happened yet. I understand what you're feeling."

He paused as he groped for his next words.

"I see Liza as a... as a beautiful young girl with a glowing face and radiant smile," he continued, looking straight into the woman's dark brown eyes. "I've never seen a condition like hers before. I am not blind. I know that it must be difficult. But I know that this condition must not have the final say.

"A few days ago, my dad saved me from drowning in the river, and I was bleeding badly after my face had hit a rock. He put some oils on my face and it stopped the bleeding and there was no cut or scar. He sent the oils with me." He again saw her cower.

"I know what you are thinking," he said. "You believe that she ... and you... will get your hopes up and be disappointed. But my father never disappointed me. I don't know what that's like. Will you, can you...trust me? Please?"

Joshua could see that he was missing information. He was used to people taking him and his dad at their word. Yet, he could see torment in her eyes and a paralyzing fear like that of an animal that has been abused. Her silence said that she would only let him get so far.

"Aqua," he said gently, "she has nothing to lose. We wash her face in the stream and put the oils on and we do not have to tell her anything. Is it you who has the fear of disappointment or Liza?"

The tears finally broke the dam of disbelief and flooded into sobbing.

"Oh, Joshua," she said, "I do believe you. I do. Oh, I'm going to wake her up with such foolish crying."

Joshua hugged the small-framed woman and patted her gently on her back.

"I'm sorry I wasn't more understanding," he said. "Oh, please forgive me. I mean no harm."

She felt so awkward crying in the arms of a youth and found his tenderness and sincerity hard to handle. Years of defensive posturing, especially in front of her daughter, had helped a soft artist develop tough skin. She kept weeping, and he kept holding her.

A couple hours later, Joshua had been filled in, and he completely understood her anxiety toward men.

"So none of the men stay with their women?" he asked.

"Well, a few," she said, "but they are the minority. They work at the seaweed factories and spend their time over there.

The townsfathers encourage that because they can have more control over the men. They hook them into town meetings after work and make them feel important by giving them positions with the city. It's company work and town work. That's their life. Girls like Liza never get to know their dads. Eventually, the men take other women and that's the way it has always been. It's such an accepted practice that Liza doesn't even ask about her father. Many of these kids end up in 'The City of Children' which is a seaside slum section with thousands of children."

Joshua knew that the time had come to reveal the reason for his stay. If not now, when? Based on what he now knew about the town and families like the Aquas, he was also beginning to have the feeling that 363 days wasn't a lot of time to get the invitations out. So, he just let it out.

"You mean," she asked, "that you put together a trip just to invite our people to your birthday party?"

"I want you to meet my dad!" he exclaimed. "He's the best host and he and the entire ranch are taking the full year to prepare, including building a huge settlement on the eastern side of the orchards. There will be a beautiful cabin just for you. It's going to be wonderful."

Liza shuffled out just in time to see her mom's astonished face.

"Did someone say something about a birthday party?" she asked as she yawned.

Joshua and Mrs. Aqua looked at each other and burst out laughing.

The youth felt the whole trip was worthwhile just to see the little girl's expressions as he retold the vision for his birthday celebration. He pulled out Sherra's homemade invitation. Liza couldn't read, but she liked the picture of the ranch with Joshua and Dad standing in front of it.

"What does it say?" she asked.

Her mother slowly read it, pronouncing one word at a time. Liza cried.

"It's beautiful," she sniffled.

"You're going love Sherra," he said. "She's nine, and she made this invitation just for you. And I can't wait for you to meet my dad!"

He picked her up and spun her around. As he looked at her face, he could see just what he had told her mom: a rosy-red complexion and an irresistible smile.

The next order of business was the bathing of Liza's face and the application of the oils. Her mother said nothing except that they were going to help her wash for a trip into town with Joshua.

In the same spot where Joshua had first met Liza, Aqua took a cloth and washed her face. While it was a bit cleaner, there was no real sign of improvement.

"O.K., Dad," he said in a whisper, "I'm just doing what you always do."

Gently applying the oils in an even fashion beginning with the girl's hairline, down her forehead and over the rest of her face and neck, Joshua stroked her hair confidently and reminded her to keep her eyes shut as he gently dunked her head in the stream.

"Oh!" exclaimed Aqua. "Oh!"

The woman wailed, frightening her daughter so that Liza immediately opened her eyes.

"What is it, Mommy?" Liza asked. "Oh, Mommy, what's wrong?"

Liza looked at Joshua who was beaming. Her anxiety eased, and she asked her mother again.

"Oh, Liza," she replied, "it's your face, my dear. Your face is rosy red. Look! Look in the water."

The girl looked where the water was calmer. She cried as the reflection explained Joshua's glee.

"It's clear," she said, "they'll never be able to tease me again. My face is as red as…"

"A pomegranate!" Joshua yelled. "You're my little pomegranate!"

They started hugging and splashing until they could laugh and cry no more. She felt new, and her face was just as Joshua had pictured it.

"Now, Liza," he said, "the children will want to know about your face. Will you keep it to yourself and be a show-off or do you want to share it…even with the ones who have teased you?"

Liza had to think about it. They had hurt her badly. They had practically chased the two of them out of town. She looked back at Joshua's eyes.

"Are you really going to hand out invitations to everyone?" she asked.

"Everyone who accepts them," he said.

"I want to help you pass out the invitations," she said.

Joshua was proud of her. He glanced at her mother, and she nervously smiled in the same fashion as her early morning mood.

"Don't worry," Joshua said to Aqua. "It's a new day."

"But it's not a new city—it's still Northcliff," she said.

"Well, let's go to Northcliff and see who accepts the invitation to Dad's ranch," Joshua said.

CHAPTER SIX

Joshua had made some room on his back seat for them, but Liza wanted to sit up front. He lent her the reins and made her promise to be very good to his best friend.

"First stop?" he asked Aqua.

"There's a neighbor who is old," she said. "He's right up here on the right, and boy, is he stubborn."

The meeting proved to be fruitless. Joshua and Liza tried to give him an invitation and a pear.

"No," he scowled. "I'm too old to travel. Right here is fine. Been here all my life. Seen everything there is to see. We old guys pretty much know what there is to know. You'll see when you get to be my age."

Joshua looked at the carriage. But Aqua just shook her head. Joshua figured that she should know. There was still time for him to change his mind. Liza didn't give up so easily.

"Look what Joshua did for my face," she said.

"Can't see that close," he said. "Well, thanks for stopping. I've got to go rest."

Liza couldn't believe her ears. How could anyone turn down Joshua? All the way back to the carriage, she threw her hands up in the air to signal her mom of her frustration. Aqua was not surprised and wondered if anyone would be open to his invitation. In the midst of discouragement, she thought about her reaction to Joshua and remembered her own cynicism.

"Maybe there's hope," she counseled herself.

"Bumpy, bumpy!" Liza cried in delight as the cart descended down a fairly primitive road. They slowed down to greet a woman with rips in her dress and a few men. Joshua felt a tug at his sleeve from the back seat.

"No, Master Joshua," Aqua said. "You must not try this woman!"

Joshua turned and looked at the worried face of his rider.

"What's wrong?" he asked. "Should I really invite one and not invite the other? I told my dad I wanted to ask everyone."

By now, the woman and the man began to notice that the strange boy was talking under his breath.

"What's wrong with you, my handsome young friend?" one of the men sneered. "You've never seen a whore this pretty, have you?"

Joshua looked at the people and did the only thing he knew to do. He jumped off the cart. Liza started to follow, but her mom grabbed her arm and gave her a stern look.

"My name's Joshua," he said, holding out his hand.

The man would not shake his hand and Joshua felt a little flushed in the face with his hand hanging in mid-air. He let it drop as inconspicuously as he could.

"I said, 'Haven't you ever seen a pretty whore?'" the man asked in a loud voice.

Joshua didn't recognize the smell of the man's breadth, but it was horrible. He just stared for a second and finally blurted, "A whore?"

The woman in the tattered dress looked down and began to walk away, but one of the others put his arms around her in a rough manner and stopped her.

"I'm afraid I don't know what you mean by a 'whore,'" he said.

Laughter erupted and a man drinking from a bottle spit it out in the air. More laughter. Joshua was not used to being embarrassed and was almost stunned by the mockery.

"A boy of your age?" snarled the man. "She sleeps with men, lots of them! She gets paid for it, too!"

Their vulgarity turned Joshua's embarrassment into a quick anger, such as he had never known. His dad had taught him to treat women with respect.

"Leave her alone," Joshua said, remembering that D.A.D. was sitting on the floor of the cart. He grabbed the stick. "I said, 'Leave her alone.'"

The man was not so much intimidated by the 12-year-old as he was the sharp stick. He took his hands off her but continued to give Joshua a look that would kill.

"I've come to give you an invitation," he said to the lady with a persistence that kept her attention. "It's from my dad and me."

Laughter was getting contagious amongst the drunk trio. But the woman stopped and stared at Joshua as if to ask, "Are you for real? Don't you know who I am?"

Joshua looked straight back at her as Liza tapped him on the shoulder. In her little hand was a big invitation.

"Here," Joshua said, taking the invitation. "I'm in earnest. I want you to come to my 13th birthday party."

He continued to explain as the background mockery intensified. She stood befuddled. All the laughing faded in her ears as she watched his lips sincerely speak to her in such a way that her eyes softened and showed another side of her tough exterior.

Two worlds were colliding in her presence. Joshua stepped toward her the way a person approaches an ambivalent cat. Finally, the invitation passed into her hands, and ever so briefly she felt the warmth of a young man who was looking to give and not to take.

Both her hands enfolded the envelope as if she was still touching his hand. She looked at it and brought the envelope to her bosom and looked back up at Joshua, Aqua, and Liza on the cart. For an instant, the drunks disappeared and all sounds and movement seemed to stop. Like a blind person receiving her sight, a blurry image of the kindness of Joshua's eyes was beginning to come into view. She could take no more. She turned and bolted down the road toward the cave in which she lived.

"Inviting whores to his party," the first man said. "Quite a precocious runt."

The others roared and headed down the road.

"Wait," Joshua yelled, "why don't you consider coming yourselves?"

"Oh no!" exclaimed Aqua. "They are violent men. Please!"

"I came to invite people of all kinds; for when they hear about my dad, they'll change," Joshua said.

"Go back to your dad and tell him that we're partying here without your help," yelled the man. "And then explain to him why you're bringing whores home!"

Dad's words of caution about wanting everyone to come reverberated in his memory. As he turned back toward the cart, he heard the boisterous group speaking so loudly that he could still hear their ridicule from the distance as they labored to walk straight.

"I'm glad they didn't accept your invitation," Aqua said in a cold voice. "Your ranch would never be the same with them."

Joshua detected the same hurt he had felt from her earlier. He did not chance to explore her anger with Liza present.

His mind reviewed the encounter with the woman.

"What's her name?" he asked.

"They call her 'Windy' because she gets around like the wind," Aqua answered. "I know her. She lives behind those trees in a cave. She used to be a different young girl until those men got ahold of her. For a split second there, I saw a glimmer of hope in her eyes. She may eventually accept your invitation."

There was silence on the cart for a while.

"Next stop?" Joshua asked after nearing the edge of the town's shanty section.

"I want to invite Cindy and her family," Liza spoke up. "That's her house there."

Her "house' consisted of some scraps of wood and tin nailed together for privacy. There was not much of a roof. A naked toddler with dark hair and brown eyes stood at a make-shift door with his thumb in his mouth.

Joshua signaled Freedom, and they stopped in front. Liza bounded out, and Joshua watched her with delight. She picked up the thumbsucker, gave him a kiss on his dirty and sore-infested cheek, and disappeared inside.

"I'm sorry for the outburst," Aqua said as she hung her head. "They've abused me as well. And Windy was never like that when she was younger."

Her honesty and vulnerability sealed their trust. He gave her a hug as she sniffled for a moment.

"I'd like to ask how these men get away with all this," he said. "But I'm afraid to know."

"They get away with it because it's written into the laws of Northcliff that men are superior to women, and we must do what they say," she said in a resentful tone.

"That can't mean just 'anything,'" he said incredulously.

"They kind of get the law to mean what they want," Aqua replied.

"I didn't think a place like this had any laws," Joshua said.

"It has so many laws that you'd break one to get to the other and not know you did either," she said. "There are laws for everything. But it's who enforces them and who knows the judge that matter. But, oh yes, there are laws. They are also tough on the few men who try to think on their own. Georgio, the man in this house, is one of them. He is Cindy's father. He does his best at the factory, but he pays for it with the same kind of treatment you just got back up the road."

"I'd like to meet him," he said as he jumped to the ground and held out his hand to help Aqua down from the cart.

Once inside, Joshua was introduced and sat with the large family on the dirt floor. He noticed the chill. There was no fire in the small hearth, and the thin walls didn't offer much protection from the elements. But Georgio, his wife Nina, and their seven kids were warm people and that more than made up for it after the morning he had just had.

"Thank you for your invitation," said Georgio in the Northcliffian accent that Joshua was beginning to understand better. "It will certainly take some doing for a family like ours to accept. I know the road you just came down is hounded by Gatekeeper, but there must be another way."

"My dad says, 'Where there's a will, there's a way,'" Joshua said. "Georgio, you know the men at work. How many are there who will accept the invitation?"

"Many men are sick and weary," he replied, "but they don't want change. It's strange. Take it from me. Every 'new' idea is cursed. It either breaks a law or it's viewed as weird. Some of my friends and I get together and talk about changing Northcliff, but..."

"But it seems impossible," said Nina in a thick accent between coughs. It was the same type of cough that Joshua had heard from the cliff.

"The men at the factory, they no good," she continued. "They sneer, they gripe, they mock my husband and threaten him when he talk this way. No good. We need the work at the factory to keep eating because they give us hemna—our seaweed bread. So what you do?"

Joshua's eyes lit up. He excused himself and brought in some produce and they all enjoyed fresh fruit and vegetables, especially Nina.

He handed her a bag of flour and yeast and explained what to do. Then Joshua felt that familiar tug at his arm, and he instantly knew it was time for him to share stories of the ranch.

"Please, Master Joshua," said Georgio, "go ahead. I'd like to hear them myself."

Joshua went on and on with his captive audience about his dad, all the hired hands, and the beauty of the ranch. The children kept asking if they could go now. Finally, Joshua put his fingers to his lips.

"Shhh," he said gently, "your mom and dad will tell you when you can go. It won't be right away."

Meanwhile, the kids were getting a kick out of the invitations that the children on the ranch had drawn. They were also begging him for some of the oils and soaps that he had used to clear up Liza's face. He told them that he would use some tonight.

Joshua couldn't refuse their invitation to pull Freedom and the wagon alongside the shack for the rest of the afternoon and evening. He took a nap on the cot that Charlie had made for him. He talked to his father and talked himself right to sleep.

Nina hadn't been feeling well and was coughing rather steadily from her cot when Joshua came back into the shack after his nap. Aqua motioned to him, and Joshua could tell something was up.

"She's gets bad sometimes," said Georgio to Joshua in a soft tone. "They call this the 'cliffhanger,' named after the town and the fact that it's a scary condition. But I know she'll get better."

But Joshua sensed his fear. He looked at Aqua and knew what she was thinking. The coughing persisted and she seemed to be fighting a high fever as well. Some of Cindy's older siblings had been comforting her because she was frightened by the worsening condition.

Joshua retrieved his satchel from the cart and returned. Liza and Aqua were waiting. He instructed everyone to gather around Nina's cot. From the smallest to the oldest, all eyes were on Joshua for they had been prepared by Liza. Georgio held Nina's hand as Joshua bathed her face with some ranch water and dried her brows with a clean towel. He pictured his dad pouring the oil on his head, and he did the same. He took a few drops and placed them under her nose. She took a few breaths and seem to gag and get worse. All of sudden, she sat up and violently spat mucus up into a bowl time after time until she seemed too exhausted to cough any more.

She looked at Joshua and hugged him as her strength returned.

"I was on death's doorstep," she said. "And yet now I breathe. How is possible?"

"When you meet my dad," he said, "you can thank him."

"I am healed!" she said, finally realizing that this was real. "I am healed!"

The children almost knocked Joshua over getting to their mom for a family hug.

"Joshua," said Georgio, "I can not tell you what this means to our family. She the heart of our home, and the heart nearly stopped beating. You've not only brought us healing, you've brought us great joy. I want to accept your invitation for your party on behalf of the Rapha family… to honor you and to thank your father for this oil and for sending you."

"You've made me part of your family," Joshua replied. "It will be my pleasure to have you be part of ours. Dad loves families and he's great with kids. Don't worry about getting up the mountain. We'll make it."

"It will be a climb," said Georgio. "But I have some ideas on how to prepare."

Meanwhile, a fire had been started under the oven and Nina was following Joshua's bread-making instructions.

"She's her old self again!" Georgio said.

"Let's get the kids around the table," Joshua said excitedly. "Come on, gang!"

Liza loved this and squeezed herself in to sit next to Joshua.

"I'm his helper," she said in her adorable accent.

He prepared the basin and oils and soap, and one by one began washing their faces.

Instantly after their respective washes, their faces were healed. The girls seemed more excited than the boys, but all were excited. Nothing like this had ever hit Northcliff. For a couple of hours, there were shouts of joy that could be heard clear down the road.

CHAPTER SEVEN

A nd it was the ruckus that caused the knock at the door.
Georgio looked into a familiar but not so friendly face of
Franklin, a poldier, who also happened to be another neighbor.

The poldiers were the uniformed guard of Northcliff. They
prided themselves in keeping the townsfathers and Gatekeeper
on the alert for defectors and slanderous types. Franklin had
turned in his share and if enough pressure was put on him, he
would turn in his own mother.

"Disturbing the peace, Georgio?" asked Franklin. "For
cryin' out loud, you can hear all the nonsense clear down at my
house. That's all I need, Georgio—all of our neighbors looking
at me as if to say, 'He can't even keep his own neighborhood in
check.'"

"Who's saying that, Franklin?" responded Georgio firmly
calling his bluff. "Why don't you come in and see what all the
fuss is about?"

Georgio had figured that curiosity was probably the reason
he came over in the first place. He knew he wouldn't normally
be in uniform this time of night. Franklin was tall and a bit out
of shape, and that fact had more than begun to show around his
bulging middle-age belly. He was rough around the edges, but
he had been known to show some heart if other poldiers weren't
around.

Franklin ducked through the door and entered Georgio's
humble domain. The last time Franklin paid a visit was the time

Georgio had said something about changing the ingredient mix at the seaweed factory. It sparked quite a controversy and Franklin was sent to tell Georgio that he wasn't the factory manager's idea of a chemist. While Georgio never let Franklin intimidate him, he was always very cautious of Franklin's presence because of his position.

"Franklin," Georgio said, "I'd like you to meet Joshua. He's come down from his father's ranch on the mountain with some great food and healing oils. Would you like to try some?"

Georgio was toying with Franklin, but it went over his head.

"Whadda I need that stuff for?" growled the poldier. He stuck out his hand uncomfortably toward Joshua.

After the routine poldier party-line grilling, Franklin seemed to be making himself comfortable as the children's complexions seemed evidence enough to Franklin that something genuine was happening. He didn't have time to process the 13th birthday party invitation or what the implications would be.

"It really is incredible," said Franklin, but then catching himself for fear that he might be encouraging Georgio, a man who was not popular with the captains of the poldiers. "Of course, there's more to life than face cleaning."

"Why don't you just take one pear home with you for you and your wife to try?" Joshua asked quickly to diffuse his tone. "And please, take the invitation as well. Your wife and children would love it up there."

Franklin departed with a pear, an invitation, and a confused mind. "What's with this 12-year-old?" he mumbled to himself as he bit into the delicious pear. He scratched his head as he made his way back down the street.

"Go back inside your houses," he snarled at the neighbors, "can't you see it's late?"

A subdued laughter broke out after Franklin's exit.

"You may not think he's very bright," said Georgio to

Joshua and his family. "But the poldiers can cause a lot of pain if you step outside the boundary of what they consider 'normal.' Please be careful with them, Master Joshua."

The sleepover cramped the little shack, but nobody minded. The girls giggled and crowded around the fire before going to sleep to catch one last glimpse in the mirror at their faces. Their appreciative hugs gave Joshua a huge sense of appreciation for his father.

"Good night, Dad," he said.

The family members who were still awake heard and echoed with an understanding "Good night, Dad."

Upon hearing their voices, Joshua wiped a tear, turned over on his side and whispered before falling off, "I'll see you in just over 360 days. I love you."

Franklin's report reached his captains, and the buzz was out. Defensive postures were so embedded in the poldiers and townsfathers that an emergency meeting was called between the captains and city officials.

"I told you," Franklin said gruffly, "he just puts these oils on the face and washes it with some mountain water he brought down from his father's ranch and their skin clears up."

"Well, what's with the invitation?" interrupted the high townfather.

"Like I said," Franklin reported, "he's inviting people to his dad's ranch for his 13th birthday party. Nobody's going to go with a 12-year-old up that mountain. They all know that the Gatekeeper keeps watch on the only safe road up the mountain. What are you so worried about?"

"Don't talk to me like that!" cried the official. "I know when to be concerned about a 'Northcliffslanderer.'" (That was the term for those who talked down their fair city and punishment was death.)

Franklin said no more. But he thought about the pear that

his wife loved so much and the healing of his own son by Joshua that very morning on his way down the road that morning. He could find no fault with the young healer. However, he hid his feelings from his fellow poldiers.

Joshua was spending a little extra time with Freedom that morning. He felt that Freedom wasn't used to the emotional competition that all the new friends were providing. He made a pact with Freedom.

"I'll take you on the longest ride on the night of my 13th birthday party," he told his horse. "I know this can't be easy for a horse like you to be all tied up like this. You're such a good servant to do this."

And Joshua made sure that Freedom felt secure from then on. The horse gave him an affectionate nudge just before Joshua went back inside.

Georgio, his family, Aqua, Liza, and Joshua set out after they finished eating a combination breakfast of Northcliffian and ranch cuisine. As they left the house, someone touched Joshua from behind. Turning suddenly, Joshua looked straight into the radiant eyes of Windy who hugged him freely and purely.

"Thank you, Joshua," she said. "I am a new person. I've read that invitation over and over again. I feel as if I'm in a new world."

She was beaming. Joshua was speechless. Aqua couldn't believe the change. Georgio and Nina stood in wonder. Finally, the two women went over to hug her.

"We understand!" Aqua said.

Joshua was trying to put his feelings into words, but they were slow coming out. Windy's ripped dress was still a bit immodest, but her countenance was innocent and fresh. He had never imagined that his trip could bring about so much good.

"Windy," he finally said, "I have a present for you!"

Freedom turned and let out a loud "neigh" as Joshua bounded up into the back of the wagon to search for something for it.

"It's O.K., boy," he said to the horse.

When he returned to the group, he was holding the most beautiful lacy and long white dress that any of the ladies had ever seen.

"One of my dad's workers is a seamstress, and she gave me a few samples of her work to take with me," he said. "But why bring it out only to show? At the ranch, white is a favored color and you'll be a graceful display of the ranch's fashion. Here!"

It seemed to Windy as if the momentum of her life had swung completely around. Every moment was better than the previous. Windy's heart was pounding as she took the dress and held it up in front of her.

"OOOhh!" cried Aqua. "Windy, you look just as beautiful as when you were young! Please put it on right away. Master Joshua, may I borrow some water and oils?"

"Can't wait!" Joshua said.

When she was ready to leave Georgio's house, she looked just like one of the women from the ranch. The children gathered around her. Again, she cried. Until now, most of the children had stayed away from her and certainly didn't venture near her cave. She bent down to hug them and look into their fresh skin and faces. Everything was new.

"We'd better get going," Georgio said. "I have some friends who are not working today, and I want them to receive an invitation. This way, Joshua."

When the entourage almost reached the bottom of the hill, Joshua noticed that there were more houses here, and it was beginning to resemble a bustling city. Horse and buggies were becoming more numerous, and they were drawing looks from all quarters. Joshua didn't realize how much he stood in contrast to the locals. But each one took an invitation, if only out of curiosity. Some smiled; some were suspicious.

Georgio led them down some alleys and finally stopped in front of a small stone house with a storefront. In the windows were pieces of fairly crude chairs and tables. Joshua thought they were primitive but pretty. Northcliff didn't have the kind of wood that graced the ranch. He made no comments about this, but chose to admire the work for what it was.

"This is my friend Eric's place," Georgio said. "He and his son live here. They take this day off each week. I hope we'll find them home."

Eric was a stocky, robust man with a round face, a balding head, and an analytical mind. He welcomed his co-worker, but gave Georgio a suspicious stare when he saw the company.

"What's this all about?" he said under his breath to Georgio.

"Eric," Georgio said in a firm and confident voice, "I want you to meet Joshua. He is my friend who came down from the mountain."

Eric put his hand out properly and looked into the deep eyes of the young man who responded, "Pleasure is mine, sir."

Georgio further broke the ice by reacquainting his wife with Eric and his wife, Margita, and the rest of the group. Every one paid compliments to the furniture maker who brought them through the showroom to a spacious workshop in the back to meet his son. Jude was a well-built, 20-year-old with brownish-red hair and a confident air about him.

"Good day," Jude said to one and all. "Have a seat. Chairs are one thing we have plenty of!"

The corporate chuckle died down quickly, and it was replaced for a moment by an awkward silence. Joshua was impressed at the size of the operation considering the father-son team only did it part-time. They both worked with Georgio at the factory during the week.

"Well, to what do I owe the pleasure of this visit?" the sincere man asked.

"Eric," Georgio said, "you and your family have been my trusted friends. We seem to come up with new ideas at work all the time. Despite what most of the other guys say on the floor, our ways of doing things are creative. And our families get along and that means a lot to me.

"When I met Joshua yesterday," he continued, "I had to bring him over here to meet all of you."

After a few minutes of this kind of talk, Eric's appetite was whetted. He asked Joshua lots of questions and constantly looked back at Georgio, who was nodding his head.

"This is amazing," Eric said. "I've heard of your dad. But what we hear is always through the eyes of the factory bosses and the townsfathers."

"You've heard of my dad?" Joshua asked. "You're the first person I've met outside of Gatekeeper himself who has."

"Sure we've heard of your dad," Eric said. "The townsfathers try to paint him as a greedy landowner up on the mountain who wants to take away our workforce. There seems to be a lot of jealousy, if you ask me. I've never heard one solid piece of evidence that would portray your father in that kind of light. Most of the men just buy into whatever the townsfathers say. They don't ask too many questions, or at least not the right ones. Some of the bosses and leaders say they know your dad and claim some sort of relationship with him. You'll see for yourself when you meet some of them. I was very young when he last visited so everything is quite a blur, but some of the older guys will remember your dad. Everything you've said about him...well, it's quite impressive to hear a son talk the way you do about your dad."

"And everything I say doesn't even do him justice," Joshua said. "Anyone who's made a handshake agreement with my dad will attest to his integrity. He smiles a lot and spreads so much joy. The kids love to be around him—I think I love children because of him. The workers at the ranch are completely loyal to him for all the right reasons."

"Now that's amazing," Georgio said, with Nina nodding in agreement. "The factory guys do things that look good to their bosses, but it's not because they're loyal to them."

"Yeah," Jude cut in, "they only do the tasks that they absolutely have to do. Just ask 'em to do a little extra and forget it."

"And it seems as if your dad encourages innovative ideas," said Eric. "Around here, it's better to keep your mouth shut. I even offered to help a couple of the older workers by giving them some furniture, and they took it all wrong. They acted like I was trying to get some furniture business going or something."

"No," Joshua said, "Dad is not like that. If you accept this invitation, I promise that no one will be wrongly motivated and treat you badly."

The rest of the afternoon was spent talking about logistics. Georgio and Eric had a way with planning and engineering, which made it hard for them to accept the mockery of their fellow workers who had infinitely less wisdom than themselves. It wasn't that they were prideful; they were simply frustrated. They wanted to make Northcliff, the factories, and the entire area a better place. Yet, the roadblocks to innovation and common sense seemed immovable.

Joshua was different. He seemed to answer all of their combined questions, even though he was only 12 years old. Could a boy of 12 have such wisdom? Was he exaggerating? Could his dad be so brilliant, rich, and humble at the same time? No one else had seen the ranch; Gatekeeper would have seen to that. The two forty-something men were thinking the same thing: Joshua didn't seem like a liar. He seemed bright, confident, and a genuinely loyal son. The alternative to accepting Joshua's invitation was spending the rest of their lives being ridiculed by men whose idea of family, fun, and professional progress was best discussed over blime—a green alcoholic seaweed brew.

"No," said Eric, "I can't talk myself into staying in Northcliff—not with an invitation such as you have offered, my young Master Joshua. Jude, would you spend some time showing Joshua around since he's had some experience with woodworking? Georgio and I must talk."

And talk they did...for hours. They recounted all the failures at the factory—in relationships and with ideas. It would be a long wait for the birthday party, but they decided it would be worth it. They would use the time to plan. If many people followed Joshua up from Northcliff, there would surely be a need for an orderly departure because there would be no easy way out. The townsfathers would manipulate their laws, the factory bosses would threaten the workers, the social fabric would come undone, and Gatekeeper would procure reinforcements.

Joshua was able to persuade them to let him sleep in his wagon while the others went back to their houses. He felt at home in the back of the wagon with Freedom nearby. He still wasn't used to the Northcliff chill, so he tossed and turned all night. At least there were no dreams. And in the morning, there was no sun.

CHAPTER EIGHT

D ay after day, the dreary weather dampened everything except Joshua's determination.

He spent most of the next several months passing out invitations within the various neighborhoods and getting to know the families. Children were especially drawn to his smile and generosity. Families similar to the Raphas and the Aquas abounded in Northcliff, although the neighborhoods varied in the city proper. Many were receptive to Joshua's invitations, but unfortunately, cynicism had a grip on Northcliff. False rumors, deliberately planted by the townsfathers about Joshua and his dad, were beginning to make inroads.

Meanwhile, Georgio and Eric set up grassroots meetings among the clans they could trust. Wherever Joshua went, people were being healed. He was enjoying popularity, which stirred up the Townsfathers Council meetings something fierce.

Trust was tenuous in Northcliff because of all the manipulations used by the bosses. Betrayal had become a commonly perfected skill. It was insidious because the workers never knew who turned them in. This allowed the bosses to reassign, replace, or just keep workers in dead-end or dangerous jobs.

Willy was one worker who was bounced around. He had been assigned a position where the seaweed gets ground into a paste for the making of the "bread." Years before, his right hand had gotten caught under the heavy millstone. This injury kept him from heavy lifting—one of his natural strengths—and limited his ability to take on many jobs.

Willy was a towering, dark-skinned man. The darker people were looked on as inferior to the lighter colored people. That was just another technique that the townsfathers and factory bosses used to divide people—especially at the workplace. But Willy never developed a hatred for the light-skinned workers, or remarkably, even the bosses . He considered Georgio one of his best friends, and it was this bond that brought Joshua and Willy together. Georgio informed Willy about Joshua's trip, his mission, and the incredible healings that had happened. Willy rubbed his chin as he listened to the details—he was ripe for picking.

Joshua saw more than a good physical build in Willy. The big man's real strength was his character.

"I doubt I will meet a stronger man in Northcliff," said Joshua, extending his hand into the enfolding palms of the large man. "Your eyes dwarf your body."

Willy looked down at the young man and trusted him immediately. Willy was well-schooled in fraudulent comments, so he knew an authentic compliment when he heard one. When he withdrew his hand from Joshua's, it felt free from the restrictive, swollen feeling he had lived with day in and day out.

"My hand…" he said in amazement, looking at it and touching it with his other one. "My hand—it's better. I mean it's just fine!" It took him a second, but he quickly realized it was as a result from shaking Joshua's hand.

"How can you do that, son?" Willy asked slowly and intently. "What makes such healing possible?"

Joshua felt a little uneasy with everyone staring at him. He cleared his throat.

"Willy," Joshua began, "love makes all things possible. I can only credit my father's healing touch. At his ranch, there is healing every day. You shouldn't think it incredible that your hand was healed. We should all think it unreasonable when pain goes unanswered."

Willy, Georgio, and the others looked around at one another, and their collective silence seemed to ask the same thing, "Where did such a young man get such wisdom?"

Willy broke the quiet.

"I feel as if I know you," Willy said in a deep, melodic voice. "Do I?"

The young man assured Willy that they had never met. Willy was intensely studying Joshua's eyes. His mind began to race ahead. How could a young man survive Northcliff's corrupt atmosphere? Immediately, he assigned himself a role as guardian for the youth. He envisioned that the factory bosses, townsfathers, and neighborhood leaders would make Joshua a target of their manipulations. They would either try to get him on their side for the purpose of using him or, if that failed, they would try to cut off the people's desire to attend the 13th birthday feast.

They all met in Eric's back room and sat in a circle. Joshua knew that his trip was nearing its end, and there was no time to lose. How could these invitations get to everyone without the help of the townsfathers? He had yet to meet any of the 13-man leadership. And what of the factory bosses? They seemed to rule commerce with iron fists.

He also had a strong desire to get to The City of Children. However, Georgio recommended that he wait until the end of his stay because that section of the city was fenced in and heavily guarded.

Georgio did suggest that Joshua make a public appearance at a neighborhood meeting. These forums were ideal ways of getting the word out.

"You must realize," Georgio explained, "that the townsfathers, factory bosses, and neighborhood leaders are all tied in together. But it may be one of the few public places where you could make a formal invitation.

It was agreed that Georgio and Eric would make the connections within their respective neighborhoods. However, they would let Joshua do his own talking because they were viewed as mavericks. Joshua would have to stand on his own.

Meanwhile, talk was getting out about the healing of the children's skin and Willy's hand. Small crowds were starting to follow him around the neighborhood. Most of the neighborhood leaders were intimidated by this and made plans to meet secretly before they would greet the young man from the ranch.

One such leader was Herman, a young and ambitious neighbor and lifelong friend of Jude. When they were younger, Herman would come over and tackle woodworking projects that Eric had set out for them. The two remained close through their teenage years, but long factory hours began to erode their "hang-out" time at the woodshop.

Herman was working his way up a ladder not made of wood. He began to gain the respect of the factory bosses who were interconnected with the neighborhood leaders. There was a tidy circle of power in Northcliff.

Herman began to intentionally distance himself from Jude and his family because of Eric's nonconformist ways at the factory. Jude began to resent his dad for this. If his dad could only "fit in" a little better, Jude's friendship with Herman and his career and social position would be enhanced. He could count on Herman for that.

But he couldn't count on Herman for an invitation to the secret meeting concerning Joshua. Herman was aware that Joshua had already met at Jude's house and, in Herman's eyes, that fact disqualified Jude from attending. Jude found out about the meeting through Herman's nephew who leaked information about a "party" at the house. Jude knew what that meant, and he was determined to go as a member of the neighborhood association.

Surprise was written all over Herman's face when he saw Jude walk into the small meeting already in progress. Jude looked straight at him and boldly took a seat. Herman gave him a polite smile as if to fake a "glad-to-see-you" look.

"Mr. Chairman," the taller, older man was saying, "I have met this young man. He's only 12. Young people throw birthday parties. But really, who among us would accept his invitation to his birthday bash? It would take several days to get up the mountain. Why are you so concerned? Do you really think the whole town is going to pick up and follow a kid? This is ridiculous. You know, I think it's odd that he came down from the mountain with all this talk about his father. We older gents met his dad a long time ago. Most of you weren't even born then. His dad wanted our workforce and promised the world to us if we would only come up and see his ranch. The townsfathers and factory bosses sent him away empty-handed. Why would we want to give up our positions to go work for him? I think most people will see it like this again. Hardly anyone will accept his invitation. And isn't that what this meeting is all about?"

The rhetorical question hardly had time to land on the ears of the attendees.

"Wait a minute," snarled the man in the front row, standing and turning to address the group. "I've met him around the neighborhood. It's no small crowd that's been 'healed.' Little girls with clear complexions. That big, black oaf's hand is back to normal. Some of us were there when Willy's hand got crushed at the factory. These are not the signs of a 12-year-old who wants to merrily invite an entire town to his dad's ranch. I think his father sent him because we rejected him, and he's trying to get our kids and some of our workers again. No, this is not an innocent birthday party—this is a takeover."

Everyone began talking at once. Herman and his dad, the leader of the meeting, were whispering back and forth to one another while the small group of people in attendance began to get unruly.

"Hold it!" barked Herman's dad at the top of his lungs.

"You hold it, Danny," retorted one of the other leaders. "Let people talk. This is important."

Danny, as Herman's dad was called by his chums, let the ruckus go on for a while. But a shoving match made him take action after a couple of guys had to separate the hot-tempered duo.

"Now, wait a minute!" Danny said. "I'm in charge here, and you're going to listen to me. Why are you losing your cool over a kid who healed some people and brought down some fresh fruit and vegetables? We can grow anything he grows. We can get people healed. Now, c'mon. Let's not lose our heads, or the neighborhood will make even more out of him. Then our towns-fathers will come and take our positions away, and they would be right to do so." He didn't say this out of wisdom, but because he knew one of the leading townsfathers was quietly sitting in the back of the room.

"Jude," Herman said. "You've met with Joshua. What do you think?"

Stunned by the invitation to speak and yet honored that he was recognized in front of the association, he stood and gave them a sketch of his meeting.

"He's not to be underestimated," Jude said. "He's intriguing. I've never heard anyone talk with such admiration and loyalty about his father. And these healings are like nothing I've ever seen. He's to be reckoned with."

The townsfather silently slipped out at that point. He had heard enough.

"Furthermore," said Jude. "I personally enjoyed meeting with him. He's into carpentry and told us about some of the wood they have up on the ranch. A furniture maker has to take a little interest in that."

Jude was expecting some laughter with that line. But what he got bordered on ridicule, and he quickly sat back down berating himself over losing respect in front of the whole crowd. Herman's disgusted look didn't make him feel any better. He would have to quickly work his way back into their grace.

"As you can tell," Herman said, seizing the moment, "we've got a serious problem on our hands when even our own neighbors seem enamored with Joshua."

Herman's tone and look toward his neighbor made Jude melt in his seat.

"We must bring him before our group soon," said Herman.

The crowd was swayed by his comments and approved his suggestion while Herman was secretly enjoying the results of his effective persuasion.

"Next Friday night, it is," said Danny.

"Jude," Herman said, "since you know him, I'd like you to make the arrangements."

"I'm sure he'll come," Jude said as confidently as he could, trying to regain his composure and some measure of respect.

Back at the woodshop, Joshua had set some dried fruits before his group of emerging followers. He had never pictured himself being the center of attention in Northcliff. He had figured he would get his invitations passed out and return to the ranch. But it was not to be. Some people's envy of him was beginning to get ugly, and those who had been healed were beginning to get abused for their loyalty toward Joshua. This fact didn't crack Joshua's spirit one bit.

"It's because they do not understand what my dad is really like," Joshua said. "They only know what their own dads were like."

"But you can't tie them up and force them to accept your invitation, Joshua," said Georgio. "Remember the poldier, Franklin? He would like your dad, but he seems to get his strokes from the other poldiers. I doubt he will come."

"You never know what it takes to push someone toward love," said Joshua. "Love does have a way of shoving people around."

Light laughter was interrupted by a slamming of the front door. Footsteps followed and then the door swung wide open.

"Oh," said Jude, "I'm sorry. I didn't realize you were all here."

"Come in, son," said Eric. "Is something wrong?"

"Wrong?" Jude stammered. "Of course not."

He paused before speaking again and looked at Joshua.

"I haven't gotten much woodworking done," said Joshua to Jude, "but I've worked on some food arrangements. Try my dad's dried fruits. The best in the land."

"You're not kidding," Jude said in a more relaxed tone as he bit into an apricot. "I just came back from the neighborhood meeting. Boy, Joshua, I'd love you to go speak to them. Some of them are getting the wrong idea about you."

"We were just discussing some of those 'wrong ideas,'" said Georgio. "To me, it's that these people are blind. Look at our children's skin."

"And what about my hand?" Willy said.

"Don't you think I know? Tell them, not me. You'll have a chance, Joshua. They want to meet you next Friday night."

"That's interesting," said Eric. "They usually only meet monthly. They've called a special meeting. Something's up."

"They won't hurt you, Master Joshua," Liza chimed in. "Will they?"

"I'll be fine, and I'll be glad to meet them," Joshua told Jude.

"Well," said Willy in a determined voice. "I'm going with you. I know these people. Jealousy is their trademark."

"They just want to understand more about the invitation," said Jude.

"What's to understand?" asked Georgio. "We're going to a party in honor of this young man and to meet a man that, the more I stay in Northcliff...well, the more eager I am to meet him."

Jude's face was red. He hadn't felt comfortable at either meeting. The night plodded on for him, and he didn't get much sleep. Over the next week, he was polite to Joshua but publicly stayed away from him for fear of Herman's ridicule.

Meanwhile, Joshua was getting to know people by their first names, and he was becoming the most popular figure in Northcliff. Word reached the townsfathers, and the factory bosses made it clear through their meetings that anyone caught fraternizing with Joshua, accepting his invitation, or promoting his birthday party would have a rough time and be bounced to a different shift.

Georgio, Eric, Willy, and those close to Joshua became the target of harassment and were assigned the worst positions and at irregular hours, which began to affect their sleep and home life. One consequence of such actions revealed itself in Joshua's earshot the night before the neighborhood meeting.

At Georgio's house, the mood was not as light as it had been when Joshua first arrived.

"Honey," said Georgio, "I'm tired. Please get the kids to help you."

"Georgio," Nina replied, "not everything is children's work. I'm beginning to miss a man around here."

"You know I have not had a good night's sleep for awhile because of the hours they've assigned me to work," he complained. "They're doing it on purpose because of Joshua."

"And it's making you a wreck, and I'm not far behind," she interrupted. "Maybe we should call off this visit to the ranch. The bosses are treating you like dirt and the closer we get to leaving...well, they're going to run you right into the ground. I can't take it anymore."

"It's only a few more weeks until we leave for Joshua's party, and I'm going to be there," he said sharply.

Joshua couldn't take it any more. He knocked on the front door. The embarrassed couple knew by his face that he had overheard everything.

"Oh, Joshua," Georgio said, "you shouldn't have heard us talking like that. We're both tired and..."

"No need to explain," said Joshua. "I've caused a stir. My father warned me about this, but somehow I didn't see it coming. I've triggered a lot of pain here, at Eric's home, and in every household that has a factory worker."

"Master Joshua," said Nina, "please take no offense. But my husband does not feel well."

"I understand," said Joshua. "You have welcomed me like a son. You have trusted me like an adult. I am indebted to both of you and your beautiful family. My birthday party is only a few weeks off now. How I wish you could come. I'd love you to experience the water, just like the jugs I've brought, but there it's so plentiful from the river and wells. I'd like you to pick my dad's pears and apples and have as many as your stomach can handle. Yet, I know now it seems like a dream, a very far off dream."

"We want to go," Georgio said, with his voice trailing off as he sank down on the primitive couch. "Maybe we should talk tomorrow before the meeting, that is if I can even go. I'm so tired."

"I'm tired, too, Georgio," said Joshua. "We'll talk tomorrow."

Nina looked down, ashamed to have been the one to derail their plans.

Joshua climbed into the wagon, exhausted and discouraged that Northcliff's most persuasive man of integrity was backing down. How many would follow Georgio's exit? He couldn't think another thought before he fell deeply asleep.

Another tussle with the Gatekeeper in his dreams suddenly woke him up. It was Freedom's stirring, however, that got him out of the wagon.

"If only you were here, Dad," he said as petted and settled down Freedom. "Shhh, boy. You're going to wake the whole clan. It's only three in the morning."

The stirring creek behind Georgio's reminded him of the "Water Song." He started humming it when an exciting thought occurred to him. He had never seen the waterfall. It had to be around the town somewhere.

"Why didn't I think of this sooner?" he asked himself. "The water can't be polluted near the falls. I saw that with my own eyes. What is with these townsfathers? They must know all about the waterfall and yet keep it from the people. Hush, Freedom, we have a middle-of-the-night ride ahead of us."

The creaking of the wagon wheels stirred Georgio, and he bounded to the front door. He couldn't see, but he could hear. Joshua had given up hope. He felt like a betrayer. What began as such a promising year had turned into a nightmare. The factory bosses had seen to that. He was starting to have a bitter heart toward the bosses, his wife, and now, even toward Joshua. He wept.

Joshua guided Freedom down the hill toward Northcliff Road, the city's main avenue. Heading clear across town, he came to where the houses thinned out. Finally, the road ended at the base of the very cliff where his father had first shown him Northcliff.

Over and over, as best as he could make out by the moonlight, he tried every path to the left of the main road. All dead ends. A few of the homes were close to these side roads and he gingerly led his horse past them so as not to awaken the residents. He finally ended up on a trail that was bumpy and overgrown.

"Strange," he said to himself, "this is the longest trail and yet...not a house anywhere to be seen." He continued on through the night and thought about the dream while he rode. Why another dream about the Gatekeeper? Maybe because it was getting near the time for his departure.

"I guess another scuffle is inevitable," he murmured.

Freedom was skillfully leading them through the bumpy road when the silhouette of a shack appeared on the right. Joshua wasn't looking to disturb anyone and carefully made his way past it. Whoever was inside had a fire going and plenty of firewood stacked on the side of the hut.

"I haven't seen that much good wood since we left the ranch, Freedom," he said. "C'mon, boy. Just a few more weeks and I'll be taking you for that ride I promised you."

Just then, Joshua heard it. He burst into tears. It had been a trying night and he had almost lost hope when Georgio pulled out. Yet there it was; as unmistakable as the first time he heard it while on the camping trip.

The crashing water had a different sound to it from the bottom of the falls. It was still far off, but he was on his way.

CHAPTER NINE

Georgio was in a sour mood for a guy who was normally as steady as they come. He made no effort to speak to his wife who already felt as guilty as a condemned person. When she went outside and saw that Joshua's carriage was gone, she felt as if she had lost an inheritance.

Hurrying back inside, she asked Georgio about it.

"Why wouldn't he go?" Georgio said bitterly. "He has healed our children and friends, brought us proof that there is a better life, and we were ready to turn down his invitation. Of course, he was right to leave."

She felt as if all the blame had been hurled at her, and she shot back, "Well," what do you want to do? Let the bosses send you back to me in a coffin? That's what they'll do! Will our children be taken care of then?"

"I can't stay in Northcliff," he declared. "There has to be this ranch he told us about. I've heard about it since my youth. Our leaders will do anything to keep us from getting there."

"You'll never make it up there even if it is there," she said. "We've all heard about the Gatekeeper. He's not going to let a big crowd just saunter up the mountain."

"Well, how did Joshua make it down here?" he said. "Where there's a will, there's a way!"

"Where there are dreams, you mean," she said. "We've all had dreams about your ideas for improving the factory. And what has become of them?"

88

"That's the bosses' fault, not Joshua's," he said. "That young man has proven to be a man of his word, and we let him go. What must he be thinking right now?"

Joshua was thinking about his dad. Maybe if he could get to the waterfall, he could shout up to the top, and his dad would be there.

Light was beginning to make its way over the top of the cliff. Freedom had the luxury of seeing the path clearly now. The sounds of the waterfall were getting louder and louder.

Joshua had chills just thinking about it. Perhaps it was because of the association of it with his dad, or maybe because of its mighty display, or perhaps even because of the cover-up by the townsfathers. It was probably all of these that drove him steadily toward its thunder.

The trees cleared and so did the view of the most spectacular sight he had seen since leaving the ranch. It was breathtaking. Even Freedom pulled up, and they stared at the awesome sight. Finally, Joshua gently tugged on the reins and soon they were at the base of the falls. Getting down from the carriage, he solemnly warned Freedom to be careful along the rocky banks. He took his shirt off and made his way into a swirling side pool where it was safe.

The water was refreshing, inviting him to go back in again and again. He was feeling like a twelve year-old once more. Northcliff seemed a million miles away and the water was clear and fresh. He felt as though he could swim all day and was deeply tempted to skip the neighborhood meeting. The only thing missing was Dad.

The guard from the hut noticed the horse's fresh droppings and immediately figured that it must be Joshua. He had been half-expecting him to arrive sooner than this, but he was taken back by the middle-of-the-night timing of the young man.

89

"A surprise attack, huh?" he said to himself. "Maybe, he's brought a whole bunch of people. I'll need some help."

Riding into town, the officer reported his findings to the high townsfather who quickly gathered the rest of the council.

"This is the perfect opportunity," he said. "Northcliff is crazy about this kid. We should take care of his rebellious soul while no one is around. It wouldn't be a tragedy if he misses that neighborhood meeting tonight."

"That's right," said Coldufus. "I was at that meeting last week. Joshua is causing division within the neighborhoods, and I have been told that he's going to visit the factories next. This birthday party of his is only a couple days away."

A couple of dissenting council members were ridiculed for their support of Joshua.

"But we should have him speak before our council," said Josepheni. "I think we should hear what he has to say for the good of Northcliff."

"What he has to say is that his dad, whom many of you met many years ago, wants our workforce," said the high townsfather. "See that he has an accident at the falls."

"There's got to be a better way," said Josepheni. "He's just a boy."

"A dangerous boy who does not like the way we do things around here," said the high townfather.

Over the objection of Josepheni and Nicholas, it was agreed to dispatch a few poldiers to accompany the guard.

Georgio was beginning to feel confused for the first time since Joshua's visit. Everything was so clear when the young boy had first arrived. There was Joshua, young and fresh, with an obvious love for his father. He had brought physical evidence of his father's love as well: fruit, vegetables, water, nuts, berries and the healing oils. Then there was Northcliff. So what was making Georgio confused now? Nothing had changed—especially Northcliff and its leaders. In fact, they had gotten worse. That should make his decision clearer, not muddled. Georgio took advantage of his day off and walked down the hill to Eric's place. Jude met him at the door.

"Dad's at work," Jude said. "They sent someone over to make sure he went to work. Very unusual."

"Nothing unusual about it," Georgio cynically replied. "They don't want your father at the meeting."

"Why him and not you?" asked Jude.

"I don't know, unless they sent for me after I left," said Georgio.

This conversation had given Georgio the idea that he needed to make himself scarce. But where would he go?

Aqua was surprised to see Georgio. Her house was the only place he could think where he could hide.

"Come in," she said. "Sit down and tell us how you are doing."

Liza ran over, hugged her neighbor, and climbed on his lap.

"Is Master Joshua with you?" asked Liza.

"Uh, no, he isn't," said Georgio. "He's, uh, busy today."

Aqua told her daughter to go to the stream and play for a while, and the little girl reluctantly left Georgio's lap.

"So what's wrong?" Aqua said. "Is something going on?"

"I'm hiding so that the factory can't find me," he said. "I think they are going to try to make me work so that I can't attend the neighborhood meeting tonight."

"That wouldn't surprise me," she said. "They control my husband...but he seems to like it. Well, you just stay here inside. I'll keep an eye out for Franklin, and I'll get a message to your Nina."

They talked about Georgio's wife, and Aqua reassured him that it was a woman's natural desire to keep her husband out of harm's way.

"If we women lose our husband," she said, "we lose our security."

"Of course, you're right," he said. "But she seems determined to stay in Northcliff."

"We'll see," Aqua said with a twinkle in her eye.

Joshua grabbed some snacks, stuffed them in his satchel, and decided to climb the cliff. He was hoping to get a glimpse of his dad or someone else from the ranch. Joshua was muscular from his woodworking and carpentry, but these rocks challenged even his strength and athletic skills. He looked to his right for an easier way and noticed a stairway-looking trail. Using it, he made it up about 50 feet and decided he liked the view and the spacious ledge where he found himself.

The cliff's north side made it a bit cool for a nap, but Joshua was tired from his aborted night's sleep and so he stretched out and fell fast asleep.

The sound of Freedom's neighing stirred him. Was this another dream? Rubbing his eyes, he looked down to see a small detachment of poldiers rummaging through the wagon.

"He may be hiding," said one.

"Hey, this is delicious," said another. "Maybe his father's ranch is real."

"Are you going to go the little boy's party, too?" teased the Captain.

"If they have fruit like this?" he replied. "Why not?"

The slap stung.

"Hey, I was just kidding," the poldier complained.

"Well, don't get wise because the townsfathers are serious about getting rid of this kid. If they heard your 'kidding,' you might end up like him."

"Speaking of that," chimed the poldier from the other wagon, "what are we going to do with this youngster?"

"We've got to find him first," the Captain said. "But our orders are to make an accident happen."

"Hey," said the wise guy, "I didn't sign up to knock off a kid."

"Oh, yes, you did," the Captain said. "You signed up to do the wishes of the townsfathers for the sake of the good of Northcliff."

"There's got to be a better way," said the other. "If we make off with this wagon and confiscate it and the horse for violating Gatekeeper's passage procedures, we could accomplish the same thing."

"That's not a bad idea," said the wise guy. "We could just say he hid out, and we couldn't find him."

"We came here to do a job," roared the Captain, "now stop eating and start looking."

Joshua knew he was in serious danger. How he wished Dad was near. He slid back from the edge into the shelter of the cliff's dark shadow. No one would find him there.

Hours later, the first poldier's suggestion was taken more seriously.

"We'll never find him out here," he said, trying to convince his captain and avoid any unpleasantness. "Let's confiscate the horse and wagon and leave the kid to rot out here. He's got to be scared or he would have come out of hiding."

"Well, I'm supposed to guard the meeting that's not supposed to take place," said the Captain. "I guess it will look better if I show up as if it's supposed to happen and act surprised when the 'young master' doesn't show up."

The poldier breathed a sigh of relief. He didn't want any blood shed any more than he wanted to look like a wimp or get himself in the dog house with the townsfathers.

Joshua buried his face in his hands and cried as he watched them lead Freedom and the wagon off. He had never been separated from his horse. No Father. No horse. No Georgio. Alone, he wept and wept.

"Oh, Father," he cried aloud, "if only you could hear me; if only you could see me."

His howling echoed through the caverns in the cliff and seemed to make its way back to him with a reply.

"My son," the echo said, "I love you and always will. Do not give up. Remember the view from the cliff."

"Dad," he screamed, "Dad! Dad! Dad!"

He wiped his eyes and scrambled down to the next level. Down and down he descended until he was at the base of the falls. Swimming to the bank, he quickly looked up. No dad. Just a cloud of mist at the top of the falls and a rainbow. But wait! A figure. Was it an illusion through the mist? It had to be dad. Waving. He could barely make out the figure. It must be dad. Joshua waved and jumped up with glee like a man on a deserted island. Suddenly, it was just mist again.

Joshua slumped to the ground and cried some more. Suddenly, a thought came streaming down as dramatic as the falls before him. The view from the cliff. His dad was seeing the view from the cliff, and he must too. It was what first spurred him on to begin his journey.

His homesickness seemed to work in his favor. He straightened up, stood and looked up into the mist, gave one last wave, and was off.

If he didn't make it to that meeting, everyone, especially Georgio, Willy, Aqua, and Nina would figure he was a quitter. He loved them too much. He started running and didn't stop. He didn't see a soul when he passed the guardhouse. The poldiers were so confident they hadn't posted anyone there. He ran with all his might toward the meeting, not knowing what it would hold for him.

CHAPTER TEN

On the way out of the factory, Willy quickly caught up with Danny.

"He'll be there," Willy told him. "Don't call off that meeting. Besides, it will be in your best interest if he doesn't show."

"You're a crafty fellow for a dark-skinned," Danny said.

But the suggestion had hit home.

"We'll keep the meeting on for your stagefright friend," Herman said.

Jude was the first one to arrive at the hall and shook hands with Danny and Herman as they arrived.

"I have no idea what happened to him," an embarrassed Jude said. "I, I went to get him, and he couldn't be found. Maybe he got scared. He's just a youngster."

"You seem anxious, Jude," said Herman. "Placed your faith in the wrong person? What do you hope to get out of an invitation to the ranch? There will always be good work right here for you."

"But what about the healings?" Jude asked. "What about the water and the fruits and vegetables? We've never seen anything like them."

"Oh, yes we have," inserted Danny. "I was alive when his father was here. Anyone with an ounce of common sense can see that he's trying to get our workforce."

"And what if he does?" Jude said. "Suppose it's better work and healthier conditions than we have here?"

"You've got an opportunity here if you're careful," said Herman, patting his boyhood friend on the shoulder. "Just don't blow it."

And with that, Herman and his dad unlocked the front door and entered while Jude nervously paced outside.

The captain of the poldier contingent showed up as expected and made his way to the front of the hall, whispered in Danny's ear, and walked to his post at the entrance to the hall.

Willy was surprised to see Georgio and all those from the hill along with Eric.

"What made you change your mind?" Willy asked. "Did Nina have a change of heart?"

Georgio hit him in the ribs with playful punch and winked at the big man. "I want to go the ranch and meet his dad and give Joshua the best present I can get together."

"By the looks of things" said Willy, "the best present you might give him is yourself as an armed guard back at the ranch. Have you seen him?"

Georgio just shook his head.

"As many of you know," Danny began to speak in a loud voice, "we called this special meeting to discuss Master Joshua's recent visit to our community. As you can see, he hasn't showed up. But we can still take questions, and you can voice your concerns."

Danny knew how to steer a crowd, and his son was quickly following in his footsteps.

Questions flowed, ranging from Joshua's father's ranch, to the healing oils, to the reasons for his visit. This was a well-prepared audience.

Danny tainted Joshua's father's last visit with the workforce issue, and, as expected, the crowd was quickly swayed. Comments, insults and innuendoes oozed out long enough to get the attendees angry about Joshua's motivation.

Georgio and Joshua's friends were hardly surprised at the way the neighborhood leaders twisted everything. They squirmed and looked at each other, but said nothing as the crowd started to get incensed at Joshua.

"This is a nice way of saying thanks," whispered Eric. "His father's oils have healed a lot of their kids faces."

Finally, Liza could take it no longer.

"I like Master Joshua," piped in the child. "He made my face get better."

The crowd hushed and turned to see whose face belonged to this minority opinion.

"What's a child doing here?" asked a woman in the second row.

"Whose child is this?" asked Herman.

"Let her talk," said Georgio in a commanding tone.

Danny glared at him with a look that spelled trouble at the factory tomorrow.

"Yes," said an older man, "let the child speak."

Danny could see that he couldn't get around it, so he tried to make her look insignificant and himself magnanimous.

"He made my face clear up and was very kind to my mother," she said. "He also brought us good food that tasted yummy and made my friends all better, too."

"That's enough," said Danny. "Thank you, young lady."

"That's not enough," cried Eric. Jude shrank in his seat at the sound of his dad's confident voice. "He made Willy's hand better with barely a touch. Is there something wrong with that? He also changed Windy's life."

"He's a little young for that, isn't he?" a coarse old brute cracked.

Eric ignored the base remark.

"He's come with an invitation to his father's ranch. What is wrong with that?"

97

Danny and Herman both tried to interject, but Eric's stern side got the best of him and he was on a roll. By the time he was done, he had listed nearly every healing and every fruit and vegetable that came from Joshua's father.

"If Joshua's father is so bad," Eric asked, "why is his food so good? Sure beats Northcliff's seaweed, with all due respect to our ladies' cooking."

Laughter erupted and it seemed to mellow out the crowd. Some had never tasted the goodness of the ranch's produce, but the ones who had, added their hearty "amens."

Danny was in a sweat, and he shot dirty looks across the room at Eric, who glared right back.

Georgio broke in.

"Neighbors," he said, "little Liza is not the only one healed. Many of your children have been touched by Master Joshua. Granted, he is young. But he came to simply invite us up to his ranch. He wants to be our friend. His father sent his son to tell us of the goodness of the ranch. This is simple. Why are we making this so complicated?"

"I agree with you," said Herman in his slyest manner. "It *is* simple. He looks down from his ranch, sees Northcliff, and feels sorry for our poor, beleaguered town. I don't want Joshua and his dad feeling sorry for me. I'm O.K. and you're O.K., too, Georgio. We have jobs, and we're all making a living. If people get up and leave, who will work the factory—even temporarily. This is a ploy to steal our workforce. His dad sent his son to offer us some goodies to entice us. Can't you see? It really is simple."

"It really is simple," echoed the voice at the back door of the hall. Heads turned as they recognized Joshua's voice. Georgio, Willy and Eric immediately made their way to him and extended their hands to him.

"It's as simple as this," Joshua continued, "my dad is a

loving man, and he wants to share what he has. How many here like to share?"

A few hands went up. The vast majority of the room remained silent and gave him a cold stare.

"Who are you, at your age, to teach us about living?" an older man sneered. "Why doesn't your father come down like a man and talk to us directly instead of sending his son? We know how to live. We like the way we live. We don't need to be taught by a 12-year-old."

Danny and Herman sensed that Joshua was hanging himself. They let him have some rope and have the floor.

"I only want you to meet my father," he said, with the meager energy he had left after his long run. "That would put an end to your questions and suspicions. I simply want you to join me for a party. Doesn't anybody like a party?"

"We like to party with people of our own choosin'," growled another man who seemed to be as ornery as the other fellow.

"We don't even have any proof that your dad is up there," snarled a cynical woman in her forties.

Willy butted in.

"Some of you have tasted the fruit and vegetables and others have been healed by Joshua's oils," he said incredulously. "What more do you want?"

"I've never seen them," the woman insisted.

"Joshua," Georgio said. "Bring some in. If ever we needed some proof, now is the time."

"Well," exhaled an exhausted Joshua, "I can't."

"See," said the woman. "What do you take us for? You shouldn't feel sorry for us. You should feel sorry for yourself. You probably don't even have a father and made this whole thing up."

The room was buzzing, and Danny allowed the chaos to go on as a demonstration of the divisiveness that Joshua had brought to their town.

Georgio whispered to Joshua. The 12-year-old calmly explained the thievery to his friends and solemnly told them that it would be bad timing to announce the corruption at this meeting. He rolled his eyes toward the captain at the back of the room who shot him a glance right back. Joshua knew he was in the den of his enemies and the best plan would be to allow Danny to bring the meeting to a close.

Finally, Danny broke his silence.

"Joshua," Danny said in a phony gracious tone, "we know you probably mean well, but we have a great city with great people. I would like you to refrain from passing out invitations to our neighborhood. This meeting is adjourned." The gavel landed on the table as fast as the terse words had fallen from Danny's mouth.

Joshua was physically and emotionally depleted, and Willy's protective nature swooped over the youngster and got him out the back door, shielding him from any more of the verbal abuse that was already being murmured about in the hall.

Joshua missed his horse and the makeshift bed that Charlie had laid out for him in the back of the wagon. Willy and Georgio surrounded him, half holding him up as they made their way toward Eric's house, the closest place where Joshua might rest. Eric caught Jude's eye, but his son looked away and did not follow the group home.

Willy felt Joshua's body slump. The youngster had collapsed. The big man put him over his shoulder and carried him through the streets to Eric's home.

"Well, young master," Eric said as he stroked Joshua's dark hair, "I wasn't sure you were going to wake up."

Joshua looked up into the kind man's eyes and continued to weep.

"Thank you, Eric," he kept saying as the woodworker held him. It was the next best thing to Dad's hugs.

They sat there in silence, holding one another. Then, it was Eric's turn to cry.

"Jude never came home last night," Eric said. "I've lost my son."

Joshua said nothing but held his friend.

"But I feel like I've gained a son," Eric continued, looking into Joshua's eyes. "I've never felt what I'm feeling now. It's all so bittersweet. These townsfolk are portraying you by using an image of themselves. And my son sees *their* image; not what I see. Like a piece of wood that you recognize immediately as something superb—this is what I see in you. And one piece must come from a superior tree. So your father must be an excellent man."

After Eric finished crying, there was silence. The two just sat on the bed as if both had just awakened from a bad dream.

Finally, some life returned to Joshua's body.

"Eric," Joshua said, "there's still the factory and The City of Children."

"Boy," Eric said, wiping his eyes. "You just never give up!"

"I know where I'm going," he laughed. "It keeps me on track."

Eric smiled.

"Master Joshua," Eric said. "Danny is one of the bosses over there. Even if we got in, you wouldn't get anywhere. It's dangerous at this point."

"I know," said Joshua. "But most of Northcliff works there, and now I'm forbidden to pass out invitations in the neighborhoods. Now the factory is all that's left, and my time is just about done down here. I must go."

"I wouldn't if I were you," he said. "You don't know these guys the way I do. Please don't go."

"Eric," Joshua said softly as he looked away, "I must go to the factory."

101

"Then I will be there," Eric said. "No matter what happens. I will be there."

He paused, and Joshua sensed something.

"I can understand if you can't go with me," Joshua said.

"No," Eric said quickly. "It's not that. It's just that Jude must not know anything about our plans from here on out."

Joshua agreed but knew somehow that it would make no difference even if Jude knew everything. He still had some invitations in his satchel, the only thing the poldiers didn't get. He had to pass out every one that the children from the ranch had made for the Northcliffians. He wanted the factory workers and the kids in The City of Children to meet his dad and to see the ranch. All the risks he had to take were worth that.

There was a celebration at the corner table of the factory dining hall. Danny, his son, and Jude were reviewing their victory. Jude joined in the laughter, but his mind felt as if it had a fence running through its center. On the one hand, he loved his dad. On the other, he never understood why his father had to get mixed up with Georgio who had a terrible reputation among the factory bosses. As far as Jude was concerned, he didn't want to be seen with his father as long as Eric insisted on having close ties with Georgio.

He was also anxious about the possibility of more trouble at the factory as he was very well aware that would be Joshua's next move.

"So Jude, what do you think?" asked Herman. "Do you think he'll still show here at the factory?"

"I think so," he replied, as if talking to himself. "When I find out the details, I'll let you know."

Herman knew how and when to push his boyhood friend. He wanted to make sure that his ambitions at the factory and in the neighborhood association would be realized. Joshua was taking on a new meaning for Herman. Getting rid of Joshua could elevate Herman above the reputation of just being a "boss's son." He would gain a reputation in his own right if he worked this correctly. Psychologically, he had Jude right where he wanted him. After all, Jude was almost at the epicenter of the conflict, and he was an excellent source—childhood friend or not. Now was the ultimate time to use this connection.

"Why don't you come over to my house tonight?" Herman asked Jude. "Some of the higher ups here at the factory are coming over for some slime. We usually have a good time. I'll tell them you're joining us. It'll be good for you to buddy-up with them. If you play it right, you won't have to worry about building furniture part-time anymore."

"Take the day off," said Danny who was in charge of the shift. "Let us know what's happening."

He winked at Jude who nodded back.

"See you tonight," Jude said, perking up a bit as he thought about his future.

Jude never saw the smiles on their faces as he left.

CHAPTER ELEVEN

A qua and Liza slept over at Eric's house while Margita played the hostess. But no one knew that she had been up all night. Margita wasn't worried about their son's whereabouts as much as she was distraught about the apparent fracture of her family. Eric and Jude had always worked hard after hours in the workshop. Perhaps the stress of the extra work hours had created some wishful short-cut career hopes in her son. After all, there wasn't much money in the woodshop.

Her daydreams were interrupted by a hug from behind. It was Aqua.

"I understand Georgio and his wife are running into the same pressures of having to choose the safe way versus the hard way," she said softly.

"Oh, Aqua..." Margita said, as the tears finally let go.

"It's all right, it's all right," said Aqua.

Standing in the doorway, Liza heard them and rushed over to join in the hug.

"I don't understand why people don't like Joshua," said Liza. "What's wrong with them?"

"Dear," said her mother, "some of the leaders say that Joshua is trying to steal the people away."

"No," Liza said. "He just has something better for them."

Margita and Aqua looked at each other.

"Out of the mouths of babes," Margita said. "You have a beautiful and sensitive daughter."

"But let's talk about your son," Aqua said as she gently signaled Liza to go to the other room. "Give him one more chance."

"Eric doesn't want him to know anything about what Joshua's plans are," said Margita. "But I can't kick him out of our home."

And it was at that moment that she heard, "Mom?"

She looked at Aqua and turned toward the kitchen. "Hello, son..."

Meanwhile, Georgio had come down and whisked Joshua and Eric and Willy away to a ravine behind Georgio's house.

"I only have a short time left," said Joshua. "My dad is expecting me, and I miss him terribly. After what happened at the waterfall and hearing his voice, I...I've just got to see him. And we've got to bring everyone and have that party. I know I sound like I'm rambling, but we have to get up the mountain. Let's go to the factory tomorrow."

"We can't draw attention to your visit," said Georgio. "No one must know."

"I'll go alone with Joshua," volunteered Willy. "Even if they try to stop me, Joshua must get those invitations to the workers. There's so many there that weren't there when we visited their neighborhoods. But, Master Joshua, it will be dangerous."

"In Northcliff, the factory is the center of our city," added Georgio. "Many see it as their ultimate security. It's more than their pay—it's their provision, their structure, their social center...their everything. If workers lose their status at the factory, they feel doomed."

"Most of them are like my son, Jude," said a somber-sounding Eric. "He is so eager to please the shift bosses and foremen, like Herman and Danny, just to get ahead."

The next few hours were spent planning the factory visit, including the shortcut through the city's city-within-a-city—"The City of Children" and "Garbage Square." None of the bosses would be seen in that ghetto, which would make for a safe passage to the factory's back entrance.

Garbage Square was the center of The City of Children and was appropriately named. It was near the waterfront and housed a sizable dump and a huge furnace to burn refuse. The scraps of waste attracted the poor of the town and rats who both fought for the same food. Between the dampness and stench of the polluted sea and the foul furnace smoke, it was the city's darkest corner. The rats were large and menacing, and the disease they spread ran through the kids as fast as the wind. The darkest side of the dump was the graveyard, if you could call it that. There wasn't enough sand and dirt to fully bury the bodies, and rumors had it that the furnace was used for more than just garbage.

Joshua was told about such things, but he could only think of his father's generosity. He tended to think about the solution without ignoring the problem.

For all the "positive" talk about Northcliff by city leaders, Joshua couldn't understand how people could allow other people to live like this. His dad would have built them shelters, even if he had to stay up every night for a year.

"Compassion!" Joshua said aloud. "You were always thinking of others. That's it. People create poverty because they are thinking of themselves. Just like love creates water and water creates rivers and rivers breed life. Whatever you plant is what grows up."

"What was that?" Georgio asked.

"Oh," said Joshua, "I was just talking to myself."

"About your dad?" asked Georgio.

"Yeah," Joshua said. "When I see the poor and think of all the plenty there is up at the ranch…"

"It must be hard," Georgio said.

Georgio's mind drifted. He wondered what Joshua's dad looked like. He tried to envision what a conversation with "Dad" would be like; how he would shake Georgio's hand... how he would react to Garbage Square and The City of Children. Would he grow to feel and talk about Dad the way Joshua did?

Georgio's mind came back to the square where he was leading Joshua along the very edge of the neighborhood. He began to watch Joshua's eyes take in the suffering. He thought that he might catch glimpses of Dad's eyes through the eyes of Joshua and catch he did. Joshua's heart melted. His eyes truly were the window of his soul, and Georgio looked straight in. Tears began to run down both of their cheeks.

But when Joshua got in the midst of the children, he turned his mind toward their needs. He shook hands and gave out his invitations. He explained what they were so that their possible illiteracy could not block their understanding. Joshua was getting a lot of attention. The City of Children had never before seen a wholesome youth.

Joshua thought of his dad every time he reached in his satchel for some dried berries to give to the children who were swarming around him as they made their way toward the dump and the furnace. The children were all younger than Joshua, because the "cliffhanger" disease had claimed most of the children before their tenth birthday.

One young boy looked just like one of the ranch hand's sons. But instead of a clear complexion, the boy had pus running from a large sore near his temple. His face was completely scabbed over. Joshua stopped and all the kids gathered around him.

"What's your name?" asked Georgio, who was watching Joshua's every move.

"I don't have one," he said. "No one ever gave me a name."

"I will give you a great name," said Joshua reaching for his vial of oil. He bent over and rubbed the oil on the sore.

"Your name is Sozo," Joshua said, smiling at the little boy.

"It's better, it's better," said a small boy to next to him. "His sore... it's all gone."

"My face," said Sozo. "It doesn't hurt. It doesn't hurt anymore!"

The commotion and noise attracted even more little ones. Hundreds of children were clawing at Joshua just to touch him or get some berries or ask him for oil.

Sozo looked up at Joshua's eyes and saw light and love for the first time. He grabbed Joshua's waist and would not let go. Finally, as the crowd around Joshua became so intense, he leaned down and told Sozo, "I have to keep going. But I'll be back for you and the other children. Tell your friends what my father's oil did for you."

"You have a father?" asked Sozo, almost puzzled.

"Yes," Joshua said. "And I still sit in his lap."

"Do you think he'd let *me* sit in his lap?"

"I know he would," Joshua said. "Just make sure you are ready to leave for my birthday party when I come to get you."

The boy finally released Joshua while Willy, Georgio, and Eric tried to buffer Joshua from the hundreds of pressing kids. By now, the squeals and shouting of the children were so loud they could hardly hear each other.

"Why 'Sozo'?" Georgio yelled.

"It means 'healing,'" cried Joshua.

An hour later, they had made their way through the smelly city-within-a-city and arrived at the base of the largest smokestack in Northcliff. The air was so oppressive from the foul furnace smoke and the open sewage that Joshua thought he would faint. He saw a guard and offered him an invitation.

"No thanks," he said curtly. "I've heard all about what you are trying to do. Our forefathers built this town with blood, sweat, and tears and now you come to tell us that we did it all wrong."

Joshua turned and looked over the sea of suffering children and pointed.

"If this is not wrong, what is right?" asked Joshua.

"They eat," said the hardened guard. "They're all right."

"They're barely dressed or fed and have no parents," Joshua said sternly. "They're constantly coughing and many are dying. And I've heard about your solution for the dying."

"Would you rather us keep them alive?" asked the guard incredulously. "You just said they don't have any parents. What kind of life is this? At least they won't suffer."

Joshua looked away and caught Georgio's eyes. They turned and left.

"Happy birthday," yelled the guard, who was joined by some other poldiers in ecstatic laughter.

Joshua ignored the jibe and stiffly walked toward the dump and its graveyard, intent on seeing what he did not want to see. Joshua identified with the children. He was a son, too. He knew what a healthy father-son relationship could be. He could almost feel it for each child there. But how would he help them escape The City of Children? There were thousands of kids. Would some be as stubborn as the adults? How would he get them to understand? Would the guards just let them walk out of the city? It would be a three-day hike to the ranch—would they be up to it?

"Joshua," said Georgio, interrupting Joshua's thoughts, "are you sure you want to go to the dump? There are things I've never seen, but I've heard. Is it necessary?"

"When I first saw Northcliff," Joshua replied, "I wept. Not because of pollution and sunless days. But because of the ranch.

I knew of what life *could* be. I must visit the pit, so they might know the mountain."

"I trust you, Master Joshua," he said. "Perhaps I was more concerned about myself."

It was too late for either of them to protect their emotions. The children pressed against Joshua, and the three men did their best to keep them from trampling each other or harming their young master.

As they rounded the back corner of the furnace, the smell matched the cries, and Joshua wept.

"Oh, Dad," he cried aloud. "I wish you were here."

"Joshua," yelled Willy from behind. "Some of those poldiers are following us. Let's see what you want to see and get out of here. They are not going to give you much time."

They went along the edge of the mound. Body parts from small children were sticking out of the mound. The rumors weren't just rumors. Joshua could see that the poldiers were only there to pick off the weakest and bring them to their end, or else the mound would have been even worse.

Joshua spotted a naked three-year-old girl in a fetal position barely breathing, lying next to a small open sewage pond. She was trying to cough, but nothing was happening. Joshua looked behind him and spotted the poldiers.

"No," he said under his breath, "you're not going to throw her into the furnace."

He picked her up. She was the lightest child he'd ever held.

"That's my sister," said a nine-year-old boy. "The poldiers are probably going to throw her into the furnace."

"No, they won't," Joshua said. "No, they won't."

Joshua had seen enough, and the poldiers were closing in through the crowded "avenue" around the dump.

"This way," Willy said, guessing what was on Joshua's mind. He hurried them toward the back gate, a large wooden structure that opened as they went through it. The little girl's brother stayed alongside Joshua and sneaked his way out.

"Have a nice day," said the poldier from on top of his guard stand as he tugged his gate rope tight. "Have a nice day."

Joshua ignored the poldier's repetition and uncovered the little girl from under his arm.

"You're fortunate they let you through, young man," said Georgio. "What's your name?"

"My name is Joshua," said the boy. "I've been sick. But I tried to stay alive to keep the poldiers from putting my sister in the furnace. She's very ill. They come and take us away."

He said it matter-of-factly. The suffering had given him a tough exterior.

"You know," Joshua said. "Joshua is my name too."

"Really?" the boy said. "That's something."

Joshua could see the boy was worried about his sister. But he also sensed that something else was wrong as the boy started slowing down.

"What's the matter, son?" Georgio asked.

"I don't think I can walk any farther," he said.

"Have some water," Joshua said.

"Here," Willy bent down and picked him up and carried him.

Joshua looked up from the factory entrance. He had never seen a structure so tall. With the exception of the barns, all of the units on Dad's ranch were just a few stories high. There was so much space on the ranch that there was no need to build up; they expanded by simply putting structures next to each other.

Joshua's mind wandered to the housing that Charlie and the crew were building for those who accepted the invitation. Charlie was on the creative side, so there would probably be some interesting twists in the architecture. Joshua started imagining what Georgio or Aqua's housing would look like.

111

"Joshua," said Liza, interrupting his daydreams, "can we come with you into the factory?"

Aqua, the other ladies, and the kids had met them nearby.

"Oh," Joshua said, "I'm afraid not. They won't allow children in the factory. But I have some treats for you and the others once you're in the park. Your mom will give them to you when you go over there."

Aqua took "little Joshua" and his sick sister under her wings. She and the kids headed for the park where Liza's pure face was of great interest to the other children. They received her invitations from Joshua and kept touching her face.

"He'll do it for you," she said. "He loves children."

And the children played with Liza the whole time while Aqua kept one eye on them and the other on the factory entrance. She was worried sick.

CHAPTER TWELVE

Georgio was right. The back entrance to the factory was clear of guards and poldiers. What Joshua and the others did not realize is that Boris, the factory chief, Danny, Herman, and Jude were expecting them at that little-used entrance. Jude had made sure of that.

"Good work," said Boris to Jude as he slapped him on the shoulder.

Downstairs, Joshua's group entered the hall, and everyone followed Georgio to the break room.

Just then, an awful crash made everyone jump.

"C'mon," said Willy. "It happens all the time. This factory ain't safe."

"Help," a man cried. "Help!"

They followed the voice down the hall. Georgio and Eric got there first. They opened the door to see a huge wooden beam lying on a worker. It had fallen from one of the slime machine supports.

Joshua ran to the trapped man. The three men went to the end of the beam, and their substantial combined strength barely moved it. Joshua joined the effort and they were finally able to roll it off the man's bleeding head. The man curled into a ball and held his head.

"Master Joshua," Georgio said. "Your oils."

Joshua pulled out one of his last remaining vials of oil. By this time, a few other workers had made their way over.

113

Perplexed and angered to see a youth administering oils to their bleeding co-worker, they shoved Joshua out of the way.

Willy stepped in and stared them down.

"Let the young man finish his work," Willy said.

His authoritative tone worked. Joshua got back off the floor and began stroking the man's hair with the oils. The bleeding stopped instantly, and the man became alert.

"Thank you," he said. "Thank you. Thank you."

Georgio, Willy, and Eric hugged Joshua and the man while the co-workers looked on in awe.

"Some kinda magic?" one asked.

"No," Joshua said. "Just healing oils from my dad's ranch."

"You're Joshua?" asked the man. "You're the one our leaders say is dangerous?"

"That's because they haven't seen you at work," said the other.

"They've seen and they've heard—they're just jealous and afraid of losing their positions," Georgio said.

"Why, I hardly can believe what I've seen with my own eyes," the first one said. "With my own eyes."

"My head was split in two and now I'm O.K.," the injured man said. "I thought I was going to die."

The healed worker looked up at Willy.

"I seen you around the factory, and I joined all the guys in their insults about your skin color... and now...you helped save my life. What did you do that for?"

"See this young man, Joshua?" Willy asked. "He healed my hand. It's only right for me to use that same hand to help heal someone else. Besides, I know the foremen and the bosses incite you against the others. But you don't have to let them anymore."

"The break ends in a few minutes," interrupted Georgio. "If you want to get there before the shift goes back to work, we'd better hustle."

"I wanna tell the guys that you all saved my life," the worker said. "Master Joshua, I don't care what anyone says. I'm gonna tell 'em. Let me go with you."

He got to his feet, gave Joshua a hug, and kicked the blood-stained timber defiantly and headed with the rest of them to the back door of the cafeteria.

"That's funny," the healed man said. "It's unlocked."

"How fortuitous," said Georgio as he opened the door. "Not as many men as usual, Joshua."

"I was hoping there would be more people than this," Joshua said, looking down at the hundreds of invitations in his hands.

"Where is everybody?" asked the healed man to the couple dozen workers.

"What are you so happy about?" asked Danny, walking through the opposite door.

Following close behind was Herman and Jude, and a gleeful Boris.

Eric put his hands to his mouth.

"Set up..." Eric said. "Set up by my own son."

Jude looked away but held firmly to his place next to Herman.

All of a sudden, some of the biggest men Joshua had ever seen got up from two of the tables in front. They carried wooden clubs that they had concealed under the table.

"Wait a minute!" shouted the healed man. "This young man just saved my life."

"What a shame!" snarled one of the men who was walking steadily toward Joshua.

"Joshua, run for it!" Willy cried.

The door behind them was suddenly filled with more factory thugs. They were surrounded.

Suddenly, Willy charged through the pack and got promptly

beaten to the ground. Georgio tried to go around them. The healed man snuck through the crowd. Eric just sat down and looked at his son.

"If you want me," Joshua yelled. "Why are you hitting them?"

Willy and Georgio made a break for it while they still could.

"Let 'em go," snapped Boris. "Better without 'em. We'll deal with 'em later."

Eric looked at Joshua.

"They were hoping to make an opening for you, but they got scared," he said. "Master Joshua, I'm sorry."

"You're a good man and a good father," said Joshua.

"Shut up, young one," said Danny. "Get out of here, Eric. Just go. Your son saved your neck. It was part of the deal. Now get going."

"I'm not going anywhere," said Eric.

"You're so stubborn, Dad," said an emotional Jude. "Just leave."

Eric looked at his son in disbelief as three of the thugs literally lifted him and put him out of the back door.

He and Joshua exchanged glances as he was being pulled away.

"I'll go find the others," said Eric.

Joshua was suddenly left alone.

"Sit down," Danny said sarcastically. "This a break room. Take a break."

"And I'll take what's in your hand," said Herman, ripping the ranch children's invitations from his hand.

"Here, come to my birthday party," Herman joked as he started passing the invitations out to the thugs. "Here, come meet my dad."

Roars of laughter echoed in the empty hall.

Joshua thought about all the workers he would not get to

reach and all of the wasted invitations. It had not turned out the way he had thought. He didn't blame Willy and Georgio. They tried.

"Don't you just wish your daddy was here?" said Boris, stepping forward while eyeing Joshua intently. He had the darkest eyes Joshua had ever seen.

"I wish he was," Joshua said. "With all your hatred, he'd still love you."

More rounds of laughter.

Suddenly, one of the men started singing "Happy Birthday" and everyone joined in. Another made a crown out of the birthday cards and placed it on Joshua's head. Joshua was speechless and beet red with humiliation.

He felt a crisp, hard smack across his face from Danny.

"Didn't I tell you not to pass out the invitations?" he said. "Just how prideful are you to think that you are going to saunter into our factory and pass them out? Are we that low to you... that stupid?"

"However," interrupted Boris, "to show you just how our fair town operates, we are going to peacefully take you to the Council of Townsfathers which coincidentally is meeting tonight."

"What do you need to meet about?" Joshua asked. "I understand you met my dad. You know he is a good man. What problem can you have with him?"

"A dad who sends his son down to us instead of showing up himself?" Boris blurted.

"He came himself and only a few of you went back with him," replied Joshua.

"So he sends his son to finish a job he couldn't?" Boris quipped.

"I chose to come down here," Joshua said.

"'Down here?'" Boris remarked. "Do you hear how condescending he is? 'Down here.'"

117

The men were incensed after that exchange, and they started ripping at his clothes and digging through his pockets.

"Lookee here," said one, "some of the vials of the healing oils. Anyone have a boo-boo?"

"No," said another, "but I'm sure we can make one."

With that, he smacked Joshua across the face, and the young man fell off the chair and onto the floor.

"Oh, my," he said, "his birthday crown came off. Let's put it back on. And here, here's some healing oil."

He threw it on the floor next to Joshua's face and the glass splintered and flew into his brow while the oil dripped down his face. The oil brought a flashback to the time he was first introduced to it on the bank of the river where his dad had brought him back from certain death.

"Oh, Dad," he said in his delirium. "Where are you?"

"Daddy, oh Daddy," said a factory guard as he lifted Joshua off the floor and started carrying him to the door.

With glass in his forehead, a bruised face and back, and the birthday crown hanging on his brow, Joshua was dragged up the street to Townsfather Hall. People along the street ridiculed him, hoping to make points with Boris and Danny, and now the more prominent Herman and Jude. Tucked behind the crowd was Aqua and Windy who had heard about the ambush from the Willy and Georgio, who had fled through the crowd, but were now ashamed.

"He's almost unrecognizable," Aqua said, as she turned away and wept. Hugging Windy, she said. "It's a good thing Liza and the little ones were taken home."

In the valley behind Georgio's home, the men who had fled sheltered themselves from a stirring wind, a soon-coming Northcliffian storm, and a flood of guilt.

The townsfathers were made up of 13 old men. When they were all very young, most of them got to know Joshua's father when he visited Northcliff. One particular townsfather, Hautias, was the grandson of the High Townsfather of that era. The grandfather had driven Joshua's dad out of Northcliff. While Hautias was young, the memories of those days were vivid. His grandfather had made it clear that Joshua's father had "stolen" a lot of the Northcliffians during that visit. He also told Hautias to remember one thing, "People will serve you if they fear you; but they will not serve you if someone else is allowed to challenge your authority or offer better living conditions."

Hautias could hear these life-directing words as if it were yesterday. As he grew up and climbed his way up the power structure of Northcliff, he crushed several people who vied for the same positions he was trying to attain. As a result, he had a reputation as being ruthless, and his grandfather's advice seemed to carry him to the coveted "High Townsfather" office, one he had held for decades.

To date, Joshua was the biggest challenge of his reign— people were ready to follow him right out of town. That hit right at the heart of the "everything-is-rosy" attitude in Northcliff.

Josepheni and Nicholas were even younger when Joshua's dad visited, and they remembered very little about the rancher. They had gotten to know Joshua over the past several months and were convinced that his father was everything that Joshua said he was. These two were the only ones on the Council of Townfathers who saw Joshua for who he was and they were determined to sway the members to hear Joshua out.

There was no small commotion when the poldiers dragged Joshua in, looking every bit like a beaten up prisoner who had tried to escape. Nicholas and Josepheni were shocked to see the young man in such a state. When the poldiers plopped Joshua down in a chair, he slumped forward.

"What do you have to say for yourself, Prince Joshua?" asked Hautias in a deep and menacing voice.

Glancing toward Nicholas and Josepheni, he continued, "I have promised this council a fair hearing of your story."

"Here's a cup of water," Nicholas said as he held Joshua's head up and made him take a swallow.

Joshua's eyes were swollen from the beating and his mind was half shut as well. He could barely see, but he could sense the hatred toward him and his father in the council chambers. He thought about what his dad would say. Then, words stumbled out of his mouth.

"My father is a good man, and he would welcome a healthy exchange," Joshua said slowly.

Hints of laughter began to surface. The gavel landed a few times.

"Here, here," barked Hautias, "let's listen to the young man."

By this time, Joshua was no stranger to ridicule. The cafeteria experience had brought him low. He figured it couldn't get much worse. So, he would make one more effort to invite people to meet his dad and celebrate the liberty of the ranch.

"I recognize that many believe that my father has other motives," Joshua said, "especially in the area of recruiting labor. But you must understand, he doesn't need laborers, he simply likes to let people explore their talents and experience the freedom of working hard at something you love."

Murmuring was going on. Some were calling an end to it.

"Let him continue," cried Josepheni.

"Josepheni, are you going to his party, too?" asked a mocking voice from the back.

"Never mind!" said Josepheni. "Just let him finish."

"He'll finish himself," whispered another.

Joshua rubbed his eyes and continued.

"The ranch is a place of beauty," Joshua said. "It's a place of inspiration. We have barns where men care for the animals like

120

Freedom. Women sew the most beautiful dresses for their daughters and themselves and make wonderful pants and shirts for the men. Their quilts are beyond description. The land itself is breathtaking. There is a river that flows through it so clear you can see the bottom of it and has 12 different types of fruit trees on its banks—apples, pears, cherries, you name it. And the grains for the bread are the freshest. My dad grows herbs and extracts oils for healing."

"Looks like he could use some oils right now," cracked one of the council members, who was barely listening.

Joshua heard it and bowed his head.

"My father is a good man," he said. "You don't know what you're missing."

At this, Hautias stood up.

"We don't know what we're missing?" he cried incredulously. "You don't know what you're going to miss. Our city has been here for what seems an eternity. My grandfather was a leader when your dad came through with his ideas. Nothing has changed. Today, I'm the leader. Life goes on, and we like our life just the way it is. Who are you to tell us about life?"

"I am one who has seen something better," said Joshua.

"Better?" Hautias challenged him.

"Much better than The City of Children and Garbage Square," said Joshua. "There's no such thing at the ranch. The children are well fed, beautifully dressed, well taken care of, and they have perfect complexions and joyous spirits."

"So you're a spoiled rich kid from your dad's ranch using many of our laborers up there to make his profits," cried Hautias, "and you mock our poor."

"I don't mock your poor," said Joshua, through stinging tears. "I say there is no reason to keep them poor and even less reason to burn them."

"Don't you get it?" shouted the bearded Archivus. "They are

121

unwanted. We put them out of their misery; we're just being compassionate."

"What kind of lives would they have?" cut in another member named Wolfus.

"You don't put them out of misery, you cause it," Joshua replied.

"I will not have a twerp talk to this council with disrespect," said Hautias.

"I came here to invite the townspeople to a celebration of my father's goodness," said Joshua, running out of steam and trying to remain conscious after all the blows he had suffered.

"You don't really know your father," Hautias declared. "We know him."

"I do know him," said Joshua. "You simply have wrong beliefs about him."

With that, Boris stepped in a slapped him so hard he fell off the chair. The council was in an uproar. Nicholas and Josepheni went to help him but were pushed aside by Boris' henchmen who pointed them to the door. Nicholas and Josepheni looked in disgust at the tall poldier, then at each other. They had no choice but to leave. And as they did, they brushed past Jude and Herman who had been listening from just outside the council chambers.

Jude felt sick inside and began to follow them.

"Hey," cried Herman to his childhood friend, "this is going to get better. You're going to miss it."

"I'm going to miss it all right," muttered Jude.

Jude began to run, almost knocking over the two older men on the way out. He sprinted down the hallway, opened the window and jumped to his death. Josepheni and Nicholas saw him do it, but Herman couldn't have even conceived that he would.

CHAPTER THIRTEEN

Eric found the others huddled in the valley. It was pouring rain and getting prematurely dark for three in the afternoon. The storm kept getting worse. The group looked like a bunch of children hiding from their parents after they had been caught doing some mischief. A young man was running down the hill toward them.

"Who goes there?" cried Georgio, wielding a club.

"It's me, Stefan," said the man.

"It's O.K., Georgio," said Eric, "he's a friend of Jude.

"I must speak to you," said Stefan.

"Where have you come from?" asked Eric. "Stefan, have you heard anything more about Master Joshua?"

"I'm afraid it's not about Joshua," said Stefan. "May I speak to you alone?"

When Stefan broke the news about Jude, Eric howled in pain.

"My son!" he cried. "My son!"

They surrounded Eric, but he would not be consoled. He covered his face, and dropped to his knees in the mud as he sobbed.

Word was spreading around town about Joshua and Jude. The women were not taking it well. Eric's wife was hidden from the news until later. Northcliff was in a literal and figurative storm, the likes of which no one had ever seen.

Franklin was one of the poldiers who had followed Joshua

through The City of Children and into the factory and had had a change of heart. He had seen Joshua heal the child and the man under the beam. Earlier, the neighborhood folks had softened him up a bit, playing to his kinder side. He was thoroughly disgusted with the mockery of justice that he had seen at the factory. He slipped away and went back up to his neighborhood where Nina directed him down to the shed in the valley.

"You'll find them all there," she said. "You're not going to betray my husband, are you? He's been through it. Please, Franklin."

"Ma'am," said Franklin. "Everybody's been through it today. I don't think I could make it any worse."

As he turned to go, she grabbed his arm.

"Franklin," she said, "I've known you a long time. Tell me the truth. Are you going to Master Joshua's ranch?"

He wished to shield her, but he accidentally blurted, "I don't even think Joshua is going to make it to his thirteenth birthday party."

With that, he left and Nina sat down and wept. She could not allow herself to become emotionally involved, even with her family at stake. Northcliff's oppression had taken its toll on her.

"Georgio," called Franklin when he reached the shed where the men were hiding. "Come out and let me talk to you."

"Get away, Franklin," cried Georgio. "We're in a bad way here and there could be serious trouble for you if you don't leave."

"If you double-cross him," yelled Willy. "There will be no stopping my anger."

"Don't worry, Willy," cried Franklin. "I'm on your side."

With that, Georgio opened the door and invited the sopping wet poldier into their headquarters. After Franklin's briefing, they hung their heads. It all seemed to go from bad to worse.

"Eric," said Franklin, "I really am sorry."

The two hugged and a healing occurred between a civilian and an authority figure that had never been seen in Northcliff.

"We'll have to go see him," said Georgio.

"You'll never get close," said Franklin.

"It doesn't matter," said Willy. "We left him once. We can't abandon him again."

Franklin laid out a plan whereby he could get them near Joshua.

"But I want to tell you," said Franklin, "the young boy is on his way to execution for treason. The townsfathers are unanimous...oh, with the exceptions of Nicholas and Josepheni. Joshua will be heavily guarded. They are probably on their way to the waterfall right now."

With that, the group quickly ran to the other side of town. Franklin led them through a restricted area shortcut. Those from Franklin's neighborhood never saw him in the same light again.

The rain continued to pour as the group settled on the bank of the waterfall. None of them had ever seen the falls, and they were amazed at its majesty and even more shocked that the authorities had kept them away from such a beautiful landmark. They also noticed the cleanliness of the water—something so close yet so far from their daily lives.

All these observations, however, dissipated when they saw Joshua's wagon across the way.

"Look," Georgio said, "they're using Joshua's own wagon to transport him."

Hundreds of poldiers were surrounding the wagon as it pulled up to the banks. There was no way to get across the water to help the young man they had grown to love. Even if they could ford the base of the waterfalls, the poldiers would surely slay them, especially after the boldness they had shown at the townsmeeting and at the cafeteria. They were marked men and their women would be fair game as well.

"Believe me," said Franklin, "there's nothing we can do but hope for mercy."

There was no such thought on the other side of the river.

Aqua and Windy, who were there already, joined the men as they huddled together. Aqua began sobbing hysterically as she watched them take the young wounded healer out of the back of the wagon. Windy put her arms around her as they both turned their heads away from the sight of poldiers slapping and punching their limp friend.

"He's so helpless," Willy said, clenching his fists. "I can't believe I'm not there with him. I..."

He gulped.

"I promised to watch over the young man," Willy continued.

It was the first time anyone had seen the big man cry.

"How could we let this happen?" he continued. "His father entrusted us with him."

Georgio stared in disbelief, and Eric came and put his arms around both of them.

The weeping of the women turned to howling that somehow made its way over the crashing water and into the ears and heart of Joshua. He looked their way. The look was so brief and yet time seemed to stand still. At that moment, Joshua's head could no longer hold itself up, and it slumped back down, his chin touching his chest. Just then, a big poldier pushed him to the ground and fastened his arms straight out along a log. They did the same thing to his legs. Grabbing the logs, four other poldiers hoisted the victim and rested him on each of their shoulders like they were carrying a coffin. They began their climb up the stair-like rocks alongside the waterfalls.

"Where are they taking him?" asked Georgio.

"They will execute him by throwing him from that ledge," Franklin said, lowering his voice. "I've seen it before. I don't think you, and especially the women, should watch."

126

"We'll watch," said Aqua. "We've been by his side since he came to Northcliff. We'll watch so we will never forget."

Franklin just shook his head.

What they witnessed was gruesome. The poldiers continued carrying him step by step. One slipped on the wet footing and almost went off the cliff himself. The detachment down below pointed their fingers and continued to laugh and mock the youngster even now. There was not a shred of remorse in them nor did they ever let up with their taunts.

It was getting hard now to see Joshua's face in the shadows of the ledges. With each step, the solemn witnesses' hearts sank lower and lower. The poldiers, who had carried Joshua, came to a stop on a fairly wide ledge. They dropped him on the ledge with a thud, and he grimaced at the pain running through his shoulders and down his back.

"Father!" Joshua cried out, "where are you? I need you."

"He's still talking to his dad," said one.

"You would be, too," grumbled the lone reluctant poldier.

"Do you want to go meet his daddy, too?" said the tall one.

"All I'm wondering is," said the hesitant poldier, "what did he do to deserve this?"

"He should have thought of this moment when he tried to steal the soul of Northcliff," said the other. "Now his own soul is being stolen."

Turning toward Joshua, the reluctant poldier bent over and whispered, "I wish I could find my way to your ranch."

"You'll make it," Joshua whispered.

"He'll make it all right," yelled the tall one, who leaned over, grabbed the sympathizing poldier by his shirt, and hurled him over the edge.

No small commotion went on below at the base of the falls when they saw their fellow poldier disappear into the water.

"What did you do that for?" the other two poldiers complained in unison. "We're here to get rid of this kid."

"See," said the tall one, "he's even dividing us. Let's just get rid of him. C'mon help me give him the ride of his life."

The three were in sour moods from the steep climb, the weight of their victim, and now the senseless killing of their friend.

They lifted Joshua to the edge.

"Wait a minute," said the tall one. "I can see we've drawn a crowd on the other side of the river. Let's use him as an example. Hold him up and let his friends get a good look at him for a minute. It'll give Joshua a moment to look over the edge, too."

He took hold of Joshua's brown hair and looked at him and then looked below.

"See where you're going?" he tormented.

Joshua looked down and was afraid. He remembered his dream about being caught under the water. He closed his eyes.

His position didn't escape the notice of the group.

"They are toying with him," said Franklin. "I know these guys. That tall one has no conscience. He's torturing him."

The wailing women got louder and even Franklin couldn't believe that the poldiers could be this heartless.

"Father!" Joshua yelled with his last breath.

With that, the tall poldier got disgusted and pushed Joshua over the edge. The weight of the logs made him spin head over heals several times on the way down.

The howling below intensified as the men joined the grieving women. But an even louder and overbearing eerie echo seemed to emanate from above.

"Son!" said Dad in wail that was like thunder. "Son! Son! Son!"

And looking up, the group briefly saw a figure at the top of the falls with arms stretched out and a voice that somehow overshadowed the roar of the mighty falls.

In an instant, though, the mist from the falls covered the top and the figure disappeared. The voice, however, continued its strange and horrified cry.

It was at that second that Joshua's body crashed into the boulders. No one could see his body flow downstream, but the discolored water caught everyone's attention.

Freedom bucked and bucked and was beaten into submission by a half dozen poldiers.

"The whole river is turning red," Georgio cried. "How much blood could be in one youth?"

"It was because his heart was so big," howled Windy. "How could they do this?"

Georgio, Eric, Willy, and Franklin just looked out over the water in stunned silence.

The voice from above, an entire river turning red, and their own hearts beaten up almost beyond repair was more than they could bear.

Franklin saw their despair and sensed that they might try to join Joshua in the river. He moved quickly.

"Those poldiers are going to be looking for us," he said. "Let's get moving."

But the shocked group just sat there on the river's edge.

"I'm not being heartless," said Franklin. "But I'm in earnest. We have to go now."

Georgio wiped his eyes and gradually stood to his feet.

"He wanted us to make it to meet his father," Georgio said. "We must."

With that, he and Franklin sensitively, but quickly, moved the others along.

"This way," Franklin said, leading them a different way down the banks of the river. "They'll be checking out the shortcut. Most of them don't even know the river path."

"We must tell our wives and friends," Georgio said.

"But we must get to safety first," Franklin said.

"I'll go," Eric volunteered.

"No," said Willy, "I'll go."

"Gentlemen," said the desperate poldier, "we all must go now. I know these men. They are going to want to throw all of us in the river so we don't tell others what just happened. If one of you must go back, you must come this way and go along the river bank and through underground waterways. It's the only way you'll make it to your houses. But you must follow me."

They numbly began their hike along the red river with a collective silence that each understood. The group, still reeling from the nightmare, finally reached good cover under some trees on the bank's edge.

"Now," said Franklin, "I've got you as far as I can take you. Hopefully, they didn't see me. I must go back. I'll get word to you as to what the townsfathers are up to. It's the best I can do. If I'm not at my post, they'll think something's up with me."

"I understand," Georgio said. "It's where you can be most useful. Perhaps you can be the one to alert my wife. Perhaps we can figure a way to round up everyone bold enough to accept Joshua's invitation."

"There's already been meetings between Gatekeeper and the townsfathers," said Franklin. "Hautias and Gatekeeper have a plan to seal off Northcliff. I'll talk only with your wife," Franklin said. "Any others would put you and I in danger. Stay here and wait for word from me or someone I send. I'm sorry I can't do anything more."

"Franklin," Georgio said, "I want to thank you. We haven't always treated you with respect and…please forgive me."

"Maybe I didn't always deserve your respect," Franklin said in his humble way. "I've tended to be a follower who tried to be tough. I think I owe our whole neighborhood an apology."

Emotions ran high as Georgio and Franklin hugged and

everyone said their good-byes, not knowing whether they would see him again.

They sat on the river's edge watching the river that had finally begun to clear from its horrible red color.

"We must figure a way around Gatekeeper," said Georgio.

"If the whole town shows up at his post," said an emotional Aqua, "they can't kill the city in its entirety."

"Let me tell you something," said Willy. "You should have seen the fire in their eyes in that cafeteria. They came close to killing us, and they said they were going to deal with us later. I think that threat included our families. They will spare no one to keep their power and their workers."

"We've got to think of something," Eric said. "We've got to!"

The people on the other side of the river were celebrating. They had no remorse for Joshua or their fellow comrade who perished at the hands of the tall poldier. The "big guy" was now a hero. They all patted him on the back, and no one cared a hooey for the guard he had mercilessly thrown over.

"There's talk Captain's gonna make you in charge of the manhunt to flush out all his sympathizers," said one, trying to buddy up to his new role model.

"I know just how to do it," bragged Big Guy as he drank from his flask of slime. "They all got invitations, don't they?"

"Ohhh!" said the admiring one. "That's brilliant."

Meanwhile, Hautias and another figure were riding in the back of Joshua's wagon with Freedom marching along as if leading his master's funeral.

"We'll give you 500 poldiers," said Hautias. "That will make it impossible for them to give you trouble."

"It better be enough," said Gatekeeper to the High Townsfather, "or I'll send some down for you."

CHAPTER FOURTEEN

Franklin made his way to Georgio's house to see Nina, who was still undecided about going to the ranch. He began to wonder if he had made a mistake when she simply sat down at the news. No emotions. No tears. She just stared straight ahead.

Franklin politely dismissed himself from her humble abode and walked up his beat as if nothing happened. He was half-hoping one of his superiors would see him manning his neighborhood. No such luck. All of his superior's were celebrating back at the council chambers.

He walked back up the steep road to see who was watching Liza at Aqua's home.

"Mr. Franklin," Liza called softly, "I'm over here."

Behind a large hedge to the side of her cottage, Liza's small figure could be made out.

"Are you here alone?" asked Franklin, taking her hand.

"I was downtown at Master Eric's house when the poldiers came and started throwing things around," she said as she started to cry. "It was terrible. Jude's mom brought me out the back door and told me to run home and wait for her here. But she never came, and I got scared and hid myself."

For the first time, it hit him that Northcliff had been permanently split and that decisions from here on out would by necessity have to made quickly.

"Liza," he said calmly and softly, "come out. We've got to get going."

The little girl trusted the big man and obeyed.

"Where are we going?" she asked anxiously.

"I'm going to take you to my house and then we need to get you to a good hiding place," he said, sensing her fear. "But don't worry. I'm going to make sure you are all right."

She held her hand up, and Franklin gladly held it as they walked.

"Where is my mom and where is Master Joshua?" she asked innocently.

"They are…all together near the river," he said, fumbling to change the subject. "But we must not talk about that right now. We must get you to a safe place because the poldiers are not happy with us."

"But you're a poldier," said Liza.

"I know, I know," he said. "But Liza, some of the poldiers are not nice men."

"Why don't they like us and why did they throw everything around at Master Eric's house?" she pressed.

"Liza," he said, "I think they are jealous of Master Joshua, that he could heal your face and give good food and that he speaks so nicely of his father and the ranch."

"Are we still going to the ranch?" she asked. "I so want to meet his dad and meet the little girl who made my invitation."

"Of course, we're going," he said.

"I didn't know YOU were going," she said.

"I didn't either until recently when I made up my mind," he said.

"The other poldiers won't like that," she said.

"That's why," he said, "you must not tell anyone that Master Franklin has helped you or any of the friends of Master Joshua."

"O.K.," she said. "Isn't this your cottage?"

"Yes," he said. "My wife will take care of you from here."

"Hello, Liza," said Dorothy, Franklin's wife. "Please come in, and I'll be there in a minute."

After she left, Dorothy grilled Franklin on the day's adventure and the risk of taking Liza into their house.

"She won't be staying long," he said. "We're going to have to round up everyone and send them to the shed in the valley. From there, we'll take our leave of Northcliff once and for all."

"Honey," she said in an exasperated tone, "if your supervisor stops in, we won't be going anywhere."

"Hush," he said quietly, putting his finger to his mouth, "say no more. Things are going to happen fast from now on. Just trust me and do what I say. Take Liza to the shed along with our kids. I'll get down there as quickly as I can."

He left as fast as he came and went straight to Eric's house, which was deserted.

Franklin became more unnerved when he spotted a fellow poldier. As he got closer, he realized the man was slimed up and staggering.

"Franklin, old boy," said the drunk man. "We really got that kid today! We really did him in. Invitations anyone?"

"Yeah, yeah," Franklin played along. "What do we do now? I haven't gotten any orders."

"That's because Gatekeeper is throwing a party at the council hall and the slime is flowing pretty readily," he said. "But word has it that we're supposed to meet at Gatekeeper's station by sundown—about 500 of us. I'm sure they'll want you there. In fact, my stomach feels a bit queasy. Maybe you could take my place."

"Sure," he said, "but they can't possibly expect that people are going to go now that Joshua is dead. Look at Eric's furniture store. They tore it up. Who's going to fight against all of us poldiers?"

"Stupid followers of Joshua," he hiccuped. "Some people never learn."

"Where is Eric's wife and family?" he asked.

"Say," asked the drunk comrade, "are you one of his sympathizers? You sound awfully concerned."

"No," said a red-faced Franklin, "I just wanted to know what happened to Eric's store?"

"Are you sure you're not one of them?" the drunken man asked, grabbing Franklin by the collar and looking into his eyes.

"I tell you I don't know what you're talking about," he said.

"I think you softened up to Master Joshua is what I think," he said.

"I don't hardly know the boy," Franklin insisted.

"Better watch your step," said the man. "Anyone caught with an invitation is doomed along with anyone trying to get past Gatekeeper's Station. Watch your step."

With that warning, the slimed-up poldier staggered up the street looking for his apartment.

Franklin finally found a neighbor who told him that Margita had gone to Georgio's shed. The hiding place was common knowledge. He began to worry that people would have their invitation on their person. He was also concerned that if the townspeople knew about their hiding place, there would be no trip to the ranch. All their lives were in danger. He fled for the shed.

"Margita," Franklin said in earnest, "It's me, Franklin. Open up. We have no time to lose."

Reluctantly, she opened up the door. Huddled in the small shed were 20 or more adults and children.

"You must follow me," he said. "They know about this shed."

Without questioning, they simply trusted the "new" Franklin. On the way up the valley, he stopped in one last time at Georgio's house as Margita tried to convince Nina that she should take their seven children to meet up with Georgio.

"I don't know, Margita," she said, "how are we going to make it past Gatekeeper and the poldiers? No one has ever done that before."

"Nina," said Margita, "I know you love Georgio and your children. The ranch will be healthy. Here, the air as well as the soul gets polluted. Look what these townsfathers did to my Jude. We must go meet Georgio quickly before the poldiers get here."

"But what then?" she said. "Where do we go then? There's no way out of town. I cannot put my children in danger. Georgio shouldn't have, either."

"He wants to go," said Franklin. "It's not safe here for him any more. The townsfathers are after him, and they'll come for you, too."

"I can't go," she said. "There's no safe way out of town. Tell Georgio I will miss him."

Franklin looked at Margita and said, "We have to go. We have no time to lose. The poldiers will be by here at any moment on their way up to Gatekeeper's Station."

Margita hugged Nina and turned and followed Franklin and the crowd.

"Georgio is not going to know what to do," said Margita. "And what about the others? How are we going to alert everyone with an invitation that their life is in danger?"

"The first thing they are going to do is protect Gatekeeper's Station," Franklin said. "It will be a while before they get to the folks who have kept the invitations."

They made their way through the shortcut and finally found the others.

Eric and Margita sobbed as they hugged and thought about Jude and Joshua's deaths.

"This is a cruel place," Eric cried, "we must get out of here."

"But how?" Georgio said. "How? What would Master Joshua have done?"

"His father," Liza said excitedly, "His daddy!"

This sparked wonder in the adults who had seen the figure at the top of the falls and had heard his voice.

CHAPTER FIFTEEN

Actually, the group had just missed Dad by seconds at Georgio's house. He and Charlie and a band of men from the ranch had wasted no time coming down the mountain on their horses.

They rode right by Nina, who had still been standing in front of her door. She had thought to herself, "Could that be Joshua's Dad?"

Dad knew the shortcut. He led his men there and then veered off the path that led farther down the river. He knew right where he was going. There was another smaller waterfall with large boulders at its base. Arriving there, he found just what he was looking for. Joshua's bruised body was still attached to the logs. While the poldiers had thought he had floated out into the sea, Dad knew better.

"Charlie," he cried over the roar of the small falls, "hold tight to this rope that's around my waist."

He waded out, slipped a few times, grabbed onto a boulder or two, and continued to make his way out into the middle of the river. It had been one year since he had seen his son face to face. What he saw drew out his deepest emotions. Joshua was dead. They had taken every ounce of life from his beautiful face and body.

Dad pulled out his knife and cut the lifeless body free of both pieces of wood. He hoisted Joshua over his shoulder and signaled Charlie to begin pulling them in. Again he struggled to stay on his feet, but his determination carried them both back to the river bank.

Dad, Charlie and the other men wept at the sight of the limp corpse lying on the ground.

Dad got up, walked over to Starlight, and pulled an empty vial from the saddlebag.

He uncorked it and went over to the banks and filled it with river water.

"Oh, my son," he said, "Oh, my son. Be healed with the same love you have shown."

And then, ever so gently, Dad began to pour the water over Joshua's head and began to sing as in a whisper, "Water comes from love; rivers from the water it sends, and through every rapid and bend, it sings the song that its lover sends..."

Dad broke down and could not finish. Just then another quiet voice continued The Water Song.

"And the waterfall roars in rounds," Joshua sang, "never ceasing to display its founder."

Dad's tear-filled eyes beheld his son's opened eyes.

"Oh, son!" he cried, "Oh son!"

"Oh, Dad!" Joshua said gently, "Oh, Dad!"

Charlie and the men stood in amazement for a moment and then joined Dad in hugging Master Joshua.

"Dad," Joshua said, "all those terrifying dreams came true."

"But son," Dad replied, "all the wonderful dreams of your heart will now come true because of your love for Northcliff. Oh, my Joshua, I am so pleased with you...taking on jealousy but not giving into it. Taking on hatred and suffering and not hating back. I saw you, son. I saw you.

"Father," Joshua said through his tears, "I missed you so badly. They don't really know you. Many say they know you and some say they know *about* you. But they don't know your heart. And when I was away from your heart, I never felt closer to it."

138

"Son," Dad said, "I was with you in your heart. I never left because you took me along. And I would love that everyone take me along. But those who hate you hate me, and they have missed their invitation. Those who have loved you; they love me."

Joshua finally managed to sit up.

"Dad," he said, "I wish you could talk to them yourself."

"I know you do," said Dad. "That's what I love about you. But I did talk to them myself and they would not listen. Then, I sent you, an exact representation of my heart. They would not listen to you. They simply want control and power over other people. You came to serve. They want others to serve them. That kind of heart cannot work up at the ranch. Just one of those people would change the entire ranch.

"No," Dad continued, turning toward Charlie, "we can only house people like Charlie, whom I trust to always serve. And those who serve never miss out anyway, because other servants serve them. It's a perfect cycle. That's why the ranch is so free, and Northcliff is so oppressed."

"It's just like I always noticed about you, Dad," Joshua replied, "you never think about yourself and are always serving others, and yet, you have more servants than anyone without even trying."

"And you have taught that to Northcliff," Dad said. "Speaking of Charlie's service, you are not going to recognize the ranch. No one has stopped working since you left. They've been sewing new clothing, preparing a welcoming banquet, and building houses like you've never seen. They can't wait to see you and welcome everyone who has accepted your invitation."

Just then, Charlie interrupted with an astonished cry, "Look!"

Hung up between two river boulders was the body of the sympathizing poldier who had been thrown from the cliff.

139

"It's the poldier," Joshua said. "I told him that he'd find the way to the ranch. We must help him."

"We'll see to that, son," Dad said.

And Charlie and some men made the rescue. Dad poured water over him from the same vial and the poldier was healed. They led the astonished poldier to a horse for his trip to the ranch.

"Oh, Dad!" Joshua exclaimed. "My friends...they're all in trouble! The poldiers are after them by now."

"Son," Dad said calmly but firmly, "there's only one way to the ranch and that's if they follow you."

"But Dad," Joshua said, "Gatekeeper will seal that gate off with all the poldiers in town."

"Well, son," Dad smiled, "we're going to let him do it. But I've got a surprise for him. Those same stairs that took you to your death ascend higher than anyone knows. You know the way up those stairs and anyone who wants to make it to the ranch won't have to face Gatekeeper, they'll only need to follow you. It's a steep, narrow stairway. But, as long as they follow in your footsteps, they'll be safe—even the little ones.

"I'll be waiting at the top to welcome them. I must go now for that very reason. We are going to trick Gatekeeper while they are still celebrating. We're going to draw all the poldiers into a skirmish up near the gate. That will give you and your friends time to ride around the town and get all those who accepted your invitation. But you must spend no extra time trying to convince those who have turned you down. Divide the city among your friends to spread the word and have them meet you before dusk at the base of the waterfalls. Then, waste no time climbing up the staircase. Have no fear. You will all be safe."

Joshua exchanged some quick hugs with the men and took the extra horses that Dad had brought down.

"Dad," Joshua said, "what about Freedom?"

"I took care of that!" Dad exclaimed. "Now, we've got to go in order to beat Gatekeeper to his own gate."

The band flew like the wind through the narrow path. Some, including Nina, saw them riding like lightning up the hilly road leading around the cliff and up the mountain.

Joshua tugged at the reigns of the lead horse in the caravan. Dad had tied them one to another. He figured that he would go up the river toward where he had seen them last. He knew he didn't have much time.

Finally, Joshua heard something that brought tears and joy to his heart. It was Windy's voice crying in the wind. He followed the sound that brought him down a slight decline to the water's edge where he saw her and gently called her name, "Windy."

Startled, she spun to see the young man who had set her free.

"Master Joshua!" she exclaimed over and over. "Master Joshua!"

The others heard her and figured she was still crying.

She ran up the embankment and hugged him like never before.

"Oh Joshua," she kept saying. "It's impossible. I saw them throw you from the cliff. But here you are! How is this possible? Tell me you're real, that I'm not just wishing this."

"It's true!" he said, as he swung her around and around. "It's true!"

Joshua had another of those moments where time stood still as they swung around again and again. He was picturing how beautiful she would look in the dress that the women had sewn for her. He was imagining the joy and freedom she would have with no one to ever bring up her past and no abusive men to take advantage of her. He kept staring at her smile as they made enough noise to attract the others.

Liza had been the closest to Windy, and she came running at the sound of his voice.

"I knew your daddy would take care of you," she cried. "I knew!"

"And he did; he did!" he said. "And he's going to take care of you, too!

"It's true!" Aqua said from up the path. "Come see! Come see! It's true! Joshua's back. Joshua is back."

Georgio, Eric, Willy, and Franklin looked at each other as if their ears had misunderstood. Still, they were drawn by their hopeful hearts and raced down the path after Aqua to see Joshua and Windy spinning in circles.

Aqua broke in and hugged Joshua with all the might the tiny woman had. The men came barging in, and they threw their arms around them until it was a group embrace. The horses neighed as they watched them spin like a bunch of school-children.

Finally, Joshua explained his healing. A sense of wonderment came over them as they looked at each other. Excitement about Dad and the ranch returned, instantly washing away the experience of the waterfall just a short time ago.

"My dad," Joshua said, "is looking forward to meeting each of you. He's so excited! But listen, we have no time to lose."

He told them about the secret staircase and laid out the plans for their exodus, giving them the strict instructions about inviting only those who had accepted the invitations. It wasn't time to invite; it was time to gather those who had accepted.

They were each assigned a part of the city. Eric and Joshua picked The City of Children because Eric could take his furniture wagon and put the tiny ones in the back. It was agreed to meet at the base of the waterfall at 6 p.m. That would give them just three hours.

"That's more than enough time," said Georgio. "We already

know who has accepted." Georgio knew that his wife was not one of them. But there was no turning back.

"Watch the poldiers," said Franklin, still cautious from his years with them. "They'll be looking for us."

"By now," Joshua said calmly, "they'll be up the mountain. They are making plans to seal off the city."

The group laughed, thinking about how Dad had made other arrangements.

Dad had his men hide out in the forest above Gatekeeper's post and just below the crest of the road that led from the ranch. Hundreds of men from the ranch were assigned for the decoy maneuver.

"Remember, men," Dad said, "when I give the signal, you are to follow me in line through the wooded trail which comes out right in front of Gatekeeper's booth. Don't break your line, just follow me. There'll be no need to spill blood. My son already did that. Pay no attention to Gatekeeper's taunts. Give him no hints as to what is going on. By sundown tonight, we'll have the biggest celebration the ranch has ever seen!"

A loud cheer and the sound of charging horses went through the woods and made its way to the ears of Gatekeeper and the 500 poldiers.

"What was that?" asked Hautias.

"You've been in your ivory-towered council hall too long," sneered Gatekeeper. "This is war. That's the Father's men thinking that they are going to come through this gate to collect their precious Joshua."

And he laughed and laughed. And all the poldiers joined him until they sounded more drunk than they already were from their premature celebration.

"Get ready for battle," cried Gatekeeper.

The task of gathering Northcliffians who had accepted the invitation was easy. The small city's word-of-mouth chain was better than bold headlines splashed across the daily paper.

Aqua, Liza, Windy, and Franklin took the Hill Street area and their neighborhood while Georgio and Margita set out for downtown and around Eric's neighborhood. Willy took some friends and went to the factory and its surroundings.

Joshua and Eric were welcomed by many young ones who remembered what he had done for Sozo. They begged him for food and healing, but the ones who had received their invitations in their hearts jumped on the wagon until there was no room left. A large crowd of children followed until it attracted the attention of The Dump and The Incinerator's guards.

"Joshua," one of the guards finally said, "go ahead and take these kids. I'm sure your father wants their diseases and all of the extra mouths to feed."

Joshua was used to the insults by now, but he still got testy whenever someone spoke mockingly about his dad.

"He'll not only want them," Joshua shot back, "he'll heal them and give them productive lives."

"Go ahead," the guard said as he turned away and spoke menacingly, "they'll never get past Gatekeeper to see your dad."

As the guard went back to his station, his superior came and asked him about the commotion. After learning it was Joshua, he looked white as a ghost.

"He was supposed to have been executed," said the superior, "how can that be? He must have a twin."

"Must be," said the guard. "Anyway, I let him take the kids because we don't have any support if they start a riot. The poldiers all went to Gatekeeper's station."

And just that easily, about one third of the children walked right out of The City of Children. The other young ones were just as stubborn as the adults and chose to stay because they had their own youth leaders who controlled them.

The faithful paid close attention to Joshua's instructions about *gathering* versus *inviting*. It hurt them to know that there was a way out of Northcliff, and so many were rejecting that solution.

"I wonder if we can try again in the future?" Aqua asked herself.

The exodus was ironically forming in front of the factory. Inside its gates, there was no small commotion about the sightings of Joshua. By this time, the group was marching toward the road to the waterfall. No one stopped them because there were no poldiers left in Northcliff to speak of. People peered out of their houses and just shook their heads.

"The poldiers will get 'em," said a skeptical old resident. "They'll get 'em good."

"You'll be sorry," his wife yelled at them.

No reaction was forthcoming from the parade. The tide had turned in their town.

For the first time since coming to Northcliff, Joshua could sense the oppression lifting off the huge crowd behind him. He shared that with his friends.

"I've never felt anything like it," Willy said. "It's almost inconceivable that there would be joy in Northcliff."

They had met their deadline at the base of the waterfall. Georgio, Willy, Eric, and some of the other men went up the stairway first and stationed themselves at various levels to protect the young ones from falling. The people were so excited, they were able to deal with the strenuous climb of the steep stairs.

Joshua led them up the secret staircase described by his dad. No one who had accepted the invitation was left behind.

Dad gave a loud shout as he exited the woods, and it stirred

Gatekeeper and his poldiers to form a line at the gate. Each had a sword in their hand and a horse underneath. To Gatekeeper's shock, Dad looked straight at him, gave a yell, and then turned and went right back up the mountain as did all of the hundreds of mounted men behind him.

Gatekeeper's jaw dropped.

"What's he up to?" asked a nervous Hautias. "What's he doing?"

"No time for questions," roared an irate Gatekeeper who really had plenty of time to answer the High Townsfather, but who was actually speechless.

Gatekeeper was fuming when the band came around a second time and a third time.

After the seventh pass, Gatekeeper ordered a detachment to report to the Townsfathers' Council Hall, where many of the city's leaders were waiting news of the doom of those who accepted Joshua's invitations.

Little did the detachment know what they would find: a half deserted town and a council that was still celebrating the death of Joshua.

CHAPTER SIXTEEN

The first thing that the ranch's newest residents felt were the warm rays of the sun, still high in the sky for that late in the day. The temperature was pleasant and comfortable. Breathing became less of a strain and not one cough was heard among the throng.

"We'll get washed in the river up near the ranch," Joshua told the crowd.

Joshua could hear the hoofbeats of many horses in the distance. He was exhausted from the day and seemingly endless climb up the secret staircase. But the sound of the horses, the smell of the fresh air of the ranch, and the sight of the Joshua Bridge with a "Welcome Back" sign gave Joshua a second wind. It truly was a different world up on the ranch!

He peered into the distance and could see what he longed to see. His father was galloping toward him at full stride, accompanied by a host of men.

"Dad!" Joshua cried as he ran across the bridge. "Dad!"

A roar erupted, "Dad! Dad!"

The noise was from the throng, and especially the weary little ones from The City of Children. They stampeded over the bridge and the noise from their feet on the bridge sounded like thunder.

"Dad!" cried Joshua.

The look on Dad's face was one of joy with some leftover intensity from the encounter with Gatekeeper.

"Son!" Dad cried. "Welcome back! Welcome back!"

He dismounted with hardly a tug on the reins, and Starlight obliged his master.

Dad and Joshua seemed to blend in a blur as they spun round and round in a wild hug.

They both wept like they had never wept before. By this time, Charlie and the band of men had caught up, dismounted and were greeting the large crowd from Northcliff. Dad and Joshua continued their hug as Dad kept stroking his son's brown hair and telling him how much he missed him.

"I am so pleased with you," said Dad, "that you would give up your life for your friends."

"Oh, Dad," he said through his sniffles, "I just did what I knew you would do."

"Like father, like son," said Charlie as he made his way to his young master. "Like father, like son." And Charlie's eyes could not hold back the delight of the truth he had just espoused.

Finally, Joshua turned toward the crowd, half embarrassed by his very public display of emotions. There was no need to. Hundreds came forward to give him a hug. The first was Windy, who unabashedly ran to the front of the line and threw herself at Dad's feet and wept while crying, "Your son, your son. Oh, what he has done!" Dad tenderly stroked her hair.

"Dad," Joshua said, "this is Windy."

"Welcome," Dad said tenderly, looking deep into Windy's appreciative soul. "Welcome to our ranch. It's good to have you. There are some creative seamstresses who have been working on some special dresses for you."

"Oh, Dad," Joshua said, pointing to Georgio, Eric and Margita, Willy, Aqua, Liza, Cindy, Franklin and Dorothy, Nicholas and Josepheni and their families. "These are my friends who stuck by me through thick and thin."

"Sometimes it got a bit thin," retorted Willy, still smarting a

148

bit from his desertion. But it did draw a hearty laugh from Georgio and Eric. Everything seemed like it happened ages ago.

"No," Joshua said. "Dad, these are the bravest souls I know."

One by one, Dad greeted them and ordered his men to get the dozens of wagons they had made ready and hitch them up.

"Our friends must be so tired and hungry," Dad said to Charlie. Then, turning toward the crowd, he exclaimed in a loud voice that they all might hear. "Get in a wagon. We have a birthday feast prepared that will give every one of you a second wind. Welcome to the ranch! And 'Happy Birthday' to our Joshua."

"Happy Birthday!" roared the former Northcliffians. Children, factory workers, neighborhood folks, and even a few of Franklin's poldier friends—including the sympathetic poldier—climbed in the wagons for the shortcut through the orchards. Joshua accepted Dad's hand and doubled up with him on Starlight.

The passengers in the wagon were in awe of the orchards, the wonderful colors of the leaves, and the fine wood of the nearby forests. Squeals of delight rang out from the children's wagons that gave the wagon riders a charge.

"It's better than I thought," cried an emotional Georgio. "If only Nina was here. I could never have imagined."

"Don't worry," said Willy. "We made it. Maybe she will, too."

"It's Mrs. Wooster!" Joshua cried as they neared the ranch. "Mrs. Wooster!"

She was on the porch waiting for her young master, and her hearty smile and red hair were like the welcome banner over the bridge. Scores of the ranch's children came running.

"Joshua!" she said. "How's my young master? I hope you're hungry."

"Oh, Mrs. Wooster," Joshua said. "I've been hungry since my last breakfast here."

149

"But," said Mrs. Wooster, looking at the wagons coming in the distance, "I see it was worth it."

All the ranch children had made cards and gave them to their beloved Joshua, who couldn't stop crying or hugging. He lifted his eyes from one hug to behold the largest building he had ever seen. Four stories high and a length that was beyond his line of sight was a structure that had been erected behind the barn.

"Oh, Dad!" he cried.

"Wondering where we are going to have the birthday party?" Dad snickered.

"I promised Windy a dress and Aqua fresh water and Eric a peak at our wood shop and..."

"Already being done, son," Dad said kindly. "I know you. And anything you want?"

"Oh, Dad," Joshua remembered, "I miss Freedom. They stole him."

"We'll see what we can do," Dad said. "But first we are going to let our friends get washed and dressed for the banquet."

He motioned to hundreds of the ranch's workers, and they divided the group so that they could bathe in a few of the ranch-made tributaries. They had never experienced such warm, clean water and their bodies and hair felt wonderful.

New clothes were given to everyone. White was the favored color. Windy, Aqua, Liza, and the other women all complimented each other. Next, Dad led the crowd in a parade past the most charming homes and cottages that one could imagine. Charlie and the crews had been busy! Each one had a special trim and the most quaint porches. And parade they did. The Northcliffians had never seen such homes. Yet, Dad had a home for everyone just as Joshua had promised.

Beyond the houses was the biggest fenced-in riverfront all-wooden playground made especially for the kids from The City of Children.

Upon arriving at The Great Banquet Hall, Joshua cut the

ribbon and walked into the largest ballroom he had ever seen. There was fresh food of every kind and wonderful aromas wafted throughout the hall. Servants stood ready to assist their master and the new citizens of the ranch. Joshua introduced Liza to Sherra and had them sit together.

Everyone poured in and there were toasts by Dad. Mrs. Wooster kept winking at her young master from her new kitchen facility and Joshua just smiled back.

"One last thing!" cried Dad, as he offered another toast. "I offer you Freedom!"

At once, a large sliding door next to the kitchen opened and in trotted Freedom. Another roar went up as Joshua hugged his dad and ran down to hug his friend.

"Dad," Joshua said. "I promised him a ride alone with me."

"You'll excuse our guest of honor for a while," cried Dad.

"I'll be right back, Freedom," he told his horse.

Joshua searched the hall, found "Sozo" from The City of Children and brought him to Dad.

"I promised Sozo that he could sit on your lap, Dad," Joshua said.

Dad looked like a proud grandparent with Sozo looking as content as he could be perched on his knees.

Everyone cheered as Joshua jumped on Freedom right there in the hall. Out he rode with a second wind until he and Freedom came to the cliff. He dismounted and sat where he and Dad had first planned the birthday party. He looked at the smokestacks and soot and cried again.

"I'm tired, Freedom," Joshua said as he put his hands behind his head and fell fast asleep.

A short time later, a sound awoke him from behind. Looking out over the cliff was Georgio with tears in his eyes.

"In my Father's house are many mansions:
if it were not so, I would have told you" (John 14:2a).

151

The Water Song

Chorus:

Water comes from love,
rivers from the water above.
Through every rapid and bend,
it sings the song that its Lover sends.
The waterfall roars in rounds,
never ceasing to display its Founder.

Verse 1:

Liquid Love, how can it be
that You would flow all over me?
Liquid Love, I am in debt
to every one of Your droplets.
Washing worldly residue—
Liquid Love, I want more of You!

Verse 2:

Rushing mighty waters flow,
increasing power as time goes.
Bare freedom brings its cleansing song
as I bathe in it all day long.
Purity pours forth its love,
springing from its source above.
Cascading until it reaches me,
there is no straining eternity.

©2002 Robert J. LaCosta

To order books or the CD with "The Water Song," fax requests to (518) 435-0020, e-mail orders to noreputations@aol.com, or mail to 5 Palisades Dr., Suite 230, Albany, NY 12205